Cue for a

Shiona Harkess &
John Eastwood

OXFORD UNIVERSITY PRESS
1976

Oxford University Press, Ely House, London W1

GLASGOW NEW YORK TORONTO MELBOURNE WELLINGTON
CAPE TOWN IBADAN NAIROBI DAR ES SALAAM LUSAKA ADDIS ABABA
DELHI BOMBAY CALCUTTA MADRAS KARACHI DACCA
KUALA LUMPUR SINGAPORE HONG KONG TOKYO

© *Oxford University Press, 1976*

ISBN 0 19 432780 9

All rights reserved. No part of this publication may be reproduced, stored in a retrieval system, or transmitted, in any form or by any means electronic, mechanical, photocopying, recording or otherwise, without the prior permission of Oxford University Press

ACKNOWLEDGEMENT
The authors would like to thank Peter Treacher of the Centre for British Teachers in Europe Ltd for his help and advice.

Printed in Great Britain by Lowe & Brydone Ltd. Thetford.

CONTENTS

	Page
Introduction	5

SECTION 1: BE AND HAVE

be (Present and Past)	A Family Tree	8
have (got)	A Map of South America	10
have (full verb)	Class 4A's Timetable	12

SECTION 2: PRESENT TENSES

Simple Present	A Railway Timetable	14
Present Continuous	Time Differences	16
Simple Present v. Present Continuous	Questionnaire	18

SECTION 3: PAST AND PRESENT TENSES

Simple Past	A Bank Statement	20
Present tenses v. Simple Past	Share Prices	22
Present Perfect	A Much-travelled Suitcase	24
Simple Past v. Present Perfect	A Passport	26
Simple Past v. Past Continuous	Murder at the Flats	28
Simple Past v. Past Perfect	Olympic Medal Winners	30
Present Perfect v. Past Perfect	Football Results	32
Present Perfect Continuous	Evening Classes in Cookery	34

SECTION 4: FUTURE TENSES

will do; *going to do*; *is doing* (fut.); *will be doing*	Don't Forget	36
is doing; *is going to do*	Royal Festival Hall	38
is doing; *will be doing*; *will be*	Holidays	40

SECTION 5: REVIEW OF TENSES

Pres. Perf.; Simple Past; *is doing* (fut.)	Puriton Cricket Club	42
Pres. Perf.; Simple Pres.; *used to*	Addresses	44
Pres. Perf. Cont.; *will be doing; will be; will have done;* Pres. Perf.	Hotel Bookings	46
Simple Pres.; Simple Past; Pres. Cont.; Past Cont.; Past Perf.; Pres. Perf.;	A Sale	48

SECTION 6: MODALS

have (got) to; *can*; *be allowed to*	A One-way System	50
can; *mustn't*; *would like*; *could*; *ought to*	A Slimming Diet	52
should; *may*; *ought to*; *might*; *don't have to*; *needn't*	Road Signs 1	54
mustn't; *be allowed to*; *be not to*	Road Signs 2	56
should; *must*; *had better*; *ought to*	Road Signs 3	58
shall; *will*; *could* (in suggestions and requests)	London Theatres	60

SECTION 7: MORE ON VERBS

Passive Voice

Conditionals

Reported Speech

Gerund and Infinitive

have/get something done

Road Accidents in Westshire	62
A Reading List	64
Letter Collections	66
A Savings Scheme	68
Your Horoscope	70
Hotel Suggestions Book	72
Leisure Activities	74
A Vegetable Garden	76
The Sensational Six Pop Group	78
Wayside Garage Ltd	80

SECTION 8: MASS AND UNIT

much; many; some; any; a little; a few
how much; how many
much; many; a lot of

Shopping List	82
The Swan Restaurant—Bill	84
Imports and Exports for 1975	86

SECTION 9: PRONOUNS

it v. there
Reflexive Pronouns
Indefinite Pronouns
Interrogative who; each other; one another

Tomorrow's Weather	88
A Publisher's Catalogue	90
Appointments	92
A Sociogram	94

SECTION 10: ADJECTIVES AND ADVERBS

Adverbs of frequency
Adverbs of manner
Adverbs of degree
Comparison of adjectives

Irregular comparison of adjectives

Newtown Tennis Club	96
School Report	98
Electricity Consumption	100
Yesterday's Temperatures	102
The Swan Restaurant—Menu	104
Examination Results	106

SECTION 11: PREPOSITIONS

of place

of place and time

A Dinner Table	108
A Street Plan	110
The Brighton Affair	112

SECTION 12: MISCELLANEOUS

Possession; ordinal numbers
Conjunctions: after; when
Partitive of; relative clauses; too v. either
Noun phrases and derived nouns
Time
Numbers

Birthdays	114
Chicken Curry	116
A List of Cars	118
Famous People	120
Television Programmes	122
A Telephone Directory	124

INDEX 126

INTRODUCTION

This book is for upper secondary school or adult learners of English as a foreign language. It is most suitable for students at an intermediate level or for advanced learners who need remedial practice in grammar.

THE MATERIAL

It contains material for practising a wide range of grammatical structures in a meaningful context. The context is provided by a map, diagram, table or other illustration on each left hand page. On each right hand page there are a number of drills and exercises practising some aspect of a particular grammatical topic.

The drills should be used to practise grammatical points which have already been presented to a class. They will help the class to gain active mastery over structures which they were previously unsure of. The value of the drills derives mainly from the fact that after initial guidance from the teacher, each drill can be carried out by the students themselves without intervention from the teacher.

HOW TO USE THE MATERIAL

Step 1
Before the lesson the teacher finds a drill on the structure he wants the class to practise. The grammatical points dealt with are listed on the contents page and in the index. When he finds the relevant drill, he notes any vocabulary the class may not know.

Step 2
The teacher either displays the visual by means of an overhead projector or the pupils look at the visual in their books. The teacher explains the visual by saying, e.g.: 'This is a bank statement. It shows us how much money Mr Perkins has in the bank.' or asks a student to explain what it is. The unknown words, e.g. 'debit', 'credit' and 'balance' are also explained.

Step 3
Then the teacher says the first part of the drill, e.g. in Drill C page 21 'How much money did Mr Perkins have in the bank on December the third?' and a student replies 'Ninety-seven pounds', the response given in the book (or written on the board). The teacher asks several questions using the same pattern, substituting in random order the various dates in the left hand column of the statement. The teacher should not attempt to explain the meaning of the pattern; this is the function of the visual. After the first few responses the teacher may tell the students to cover up the right hand page and look only at the visual. (If the visual is being displayed by an overhead projector, the teacher can simply erase the written model from the board.)

Step 4
The students ask each other the questions. This is the most valuable stage of the drill and should begin as soon as the class are able to move on to it. The teacher should aim to have everyone in the class using the pattern but should call a halt before boredom sets in. If the teacher feels an intermediate stage is necessary, the pupils can ask the teacher questions before going on to pupil to pupil work.

Step 5
Most drills are followed by a written exercise, although the teacher may feel the oral practice is enough. First the pupils look at the first sentence of the exercise in their books, e.g. Exercise C on page 21:
  1 Mr Perkins had £97 in the bank on December 3rd.
Then the teacher says: 'Say a sentence with December 14th', or 'Say a different sentence', and the pupils say three of four sentences using the same pattern to show them what is required in the exercise. Then the teacher tells the pupils to write the sentences down. If the teacher wants to control which sentences are written, he can write a number of cues on the board, in this case a list of dates, which the pupils follow when writing the exercise. The pupils should not be asked to write too many sentences, especially where an exercise involves fairly long sentences.

FURTHER EXPLOITATION OF THE MATERIAL

Many teachers will doubtless be able to construct other drills for which a particular visual provides a context. Although the material has been divided into grammatical topics for the convenience of the teacher, most visuals can be used to practise a variety of grammatical points or conversational exchanges. 'A Sale', for example, on page 48, could also be used to practise the passive voice:
  How much have those shoes been reduced?
  One pound.
or to practise the construction 'could have' by means of the following exchange:
  What a pity you bought that shirt last week!
  I wish I had waited until the sale. I could have saved one pound fifty.

A FAMILY TREE

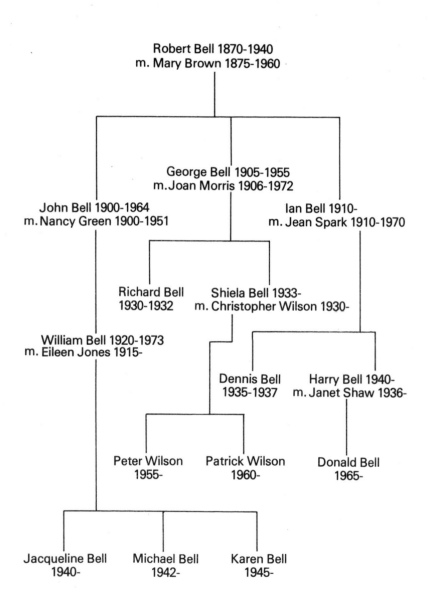

Drill A

Who is Janet?
   She's Harry's wife.
Who is ....?
   He's/She's .... 's ....

Exercise A

1 Janet is Harry's wife.
2 Michael is ....

Drill B

Are Janet and Ian related?
   Yes, they are. Janet is Ian's daughter-in-law.
Were John and George related?
   Yes, they were. John was George's brother.
Are/Were .... and .... related?
   Yes, they are/were. .... is/was .... 's ....

Exercise B

1 Janet is Ian's daughter-in-law.
2 John was ....

A Map of South America

Drill A

Has Bolivia got a border with Paraguay?
  Yes, it has.
Does Colombia have a border with Guiana?
  No, it doesn't.
Has .... got/Does .... have a border with ....?
  Yes/No, it has/hasn't/does/doesn't.

Exercise A

1 Bolivia has got a border with Paraguay.
2 Colombia doesn't have ....

Drill B

Tell me a town on the east coast of Chile.
  Chile hasn't got an east coast.
Tell me a town on the north coast of Uruguay.
  Uruguay doesn't have a north coast.
Tell me a town on the .... coast of ....
  .... hasn't got/doesn't have a/an .... coast.

Exercise B

1 Chile hasn't got an east coast.
2 Uruguay doesn't have ....

Note: *In British English 'hasn't got' is used more often than 'doesn't have'. In American English 'doesn't have' is normally used.*

CLASS 4A'S TIMETABLE

	Mon.	Tues.	Weds.	Thurs.	Fri.
1. 9.20-10.05	Geog.	Art	Music	Maths	French
2. 10.05-10.50	Science	Art	Relig.	Hist.	English
3. 11.10-11.55	Relig.	English	Geog.	French	Maths
4. 11.55-12.40	Hist.	English	French	English	Geog.
5. 2.00-2.45	Maths	Sport	English	Science	Science
6. 2.45-3.30	French	Sport	Maths	Science	Science
7. 3.30-4.15	French	Sport	Maths	Hist.	Music

Drill A

What do you have in the first lesson on Wednesday?
....

What do you have in the .... lesson on ....?
....

Exercise A

1 In the first lesson on Wednesday we have ....
2 In the third lesson on Thursday ....

Drill B

You had sport yesterday, didn't you?
No, we don't have sport on ....
You had .... yesterday, didn't you?
No, we don't have .... on ....

Exercise B

1 We didn't have sport yesterday. We don't have it on ....

Drill C

Have you got your maths book with you today?
No, we aren't having maths today.

Have you got your history book with you today?
Yes, we're having history in the .... lesson.

Have you got your .... with you today?
Yes/No, we're having/aren't having .... in the .... lesson/today.

Exercise C

1 I haven't got my maths book with me today because we aren't having maths.
2 I've got my history book with me today because we're having history in the ....

A Railway Timetable

King's Cross	13 20	13 30	15 25	16 05	17 05	17 30	19 00
Peterborough		14 40			18 13		20 13
Grantham		15 09			18 41		
Doncaster	15 43	15 59	17 47	18 18	19 28		21 33
Wakefield	16 08	16 23	18 13	18 41	19 15	20 03	21 58
Leeds	16 29	16 44	18 33		20 11	20 22	22 19
New Pudsey	16 50		18 56	19 01	20 36		22 42
Bradford	17 01		19 07	19 15	20 47		22 53

Drill A

What time does the one twenty get to Leeds?
Four twenty-nine.

What time does the .... get to ....?
....

Exercise A

1 The 13.20 train arrives in Leeds at 16.29.

2 The 17.05 ....

Drill B

Does the one thirty stop at Peterborough?
Yes, it does.

Does the five thirty go through to Bradford?
No, it doesn't.

Does the .... stop at/go through to .... ?
Yes/No, it does/doesn't.

Exercise B

1 The 13.30 train stops at Peterborough.

2 **The 17.30 train doesn't go through to** ....

Time Differences

PAGO PAGO	-11	13.00	1 p.m.
HONOLULU	-10	14.00	2 p.m.
SAN FRANCISCO	-8	16.00	4 p.m.
MEXICO CITY	-6	18.00	6 p.m.
NEW YORK	-5	19.00	7 p.m.
RIO DE JANEIRO	-3	21.00	9 p.m.
LONDON	G.M.T.	00.00	midnight
MOSCOW	+3	03.00	3 a.m.
BANGKOK	+7	07.00	7 a.m.
TOKYO	+9	09.00	9 a.m.
MELBOURNE	+11	11.00	11 a.m.

Drill A

Ladies and gentlemen, this is your captain speaking. I hope you're enjoying your flight. We're now flying over Rio de Janeiro. The local time is nine p.m.

Ladies and gentlemen, this is your captain speaking. I hope you're enjoying your flight. We're now flying over .... The local time is ....

Exercise A

1 It is 9 p.m. The captain is telling us that we are flying over Rio de Janeiro.

2 It is 7 a.m. ....

Drill B

When people are going to bed in London, what are they doing in Pago Pago?
    Having lunch.

When people are going to bed in London, what are they doing in Moscow?
    Sleeping.

When people are .... in ...., what are they doing in ....?
    ....

Exercise B

1 When people are going to bed in London, they're having lunch in Pago Pago.

2 When people ....

Drill C

Why are you putting your watch back?
    We're flying over New York and that's five hours behind London.

Why are you putting your watch forward?
    We're flying over Moscow and that's three hours ahead of London.

Why are you putting your watch back/forward?
    We're flying over .... and that's .... behind/ahead of London.

QUESTIONNAIRE

The British Tourist Board
Questionnaire for Visitors to London

Saturday April 4th 1976

NAME	NATIONALITY	PROFESSION	PURPOSE OF VISIT	ACCOMMODATION
Dr Adekunle	Nigerian	Engineer	Attend a conference	University
Mr & Mrs Jackson	Australian	Farmer	Visit relatives	relatives
Mrs MacDonald	Scottish	Shopkeeper	do some shopping	friends
Miss Pleuser	German	Musician	Play in a concert	hotel
Mr Soriaki	Japanese	businessman	open a new factory	hotel
Mr O'Neill	Irish	motor mechanic	look for a job	a friend
Mr Smith	English	builder	go to an interview	boarding house
Mr & Mrs Duval	French	school teachers	visit the museums	hotel
Miss Owens	Welsh	author	attend a wedding	relatives
Mr & Mrs Peters	Dutch	salesman	visit the Motor Show	hotel

Drill A

Where does Dr Adekunle come from?
  Nigeria.
Where does/do .... come from?
  ....

Exercise A

1 Dr Adekunle comes from Nigeria.
2 Mr and Mrs Jackson ....

Drill B

D'you live in London, Mrs MacDonald?
  No, I don't. I'm just doing some shopping here.
D'you live in London ....?
  No, I/we don't. I'm/We're just .... here.

Exercise B

1 Mrs Macdonald doesn't live in London. She's just doing some shopping.
2 Miss Pleuser ....

Drill C

Are Mr and Mrs Duval staying at a hotel?
  Yes, they are.
Is Miss Owens staying at a hotel?
  No, she isn't; she's staying with relatives.
Is/Are .... staying at a hotel?
  ....

Exercise C

1 Mr and Mrs Duval are staying at a hotel.
2 Miss Owens ....

Drill D

Mr Soriaki's a businessman, isn't he?
  Yes, he manufactures television sets.
Oh, does he? What's he doing in London?
  I think he's opening a new factory.
.... 's a ...., isn't he/she?
  Yes, he/she ....
Oh, does he/she? What's he/she doing in London?
  I think he's/she's ....

Exercise D

1 Mr Soriaki, a businessman who manufactures television sets, is opening a new factory.
2 Mrs MacDonald, a shopkeeper who sells food ....

Section 2

A Bank Statement

Mr G. Perkins
Account No. 37748246

In account with
WESTLAND BANK LIMITED

Date	Debit	Credit	Balance
3 DEC			97.00
7 DEC	10.00 Cash		87.00
8 DEC		20.00	107.00
9 DEC	34.00 Mr P. Williams		
	10.00 Foodmarkets Ltd		63.00
14 DEC	15.00 Cash		48.00
16 DEC	36.00 Bell's Furniture Store	30.00	42.00
17 DEC		25.00	67.00
20 DEC	22.00 Northern Electricity		45.00
22 DEC		120.00	165.00
23 DEC	40.00 Cash		
	25.00 Mr J. Turner		100.00
28 DEC	13.00 Mr T. Plumber		87.00
1 JAN		8.00	95.00
5 JAN	20.00 Cash		75.00
6 JAN	15.00 Smith's Garage	20.00	80.00
12 JAN	12.00 Cash		68.00

Drill A

What did Mr Perkins do on December the fourteenth?
He cashed a cheque for fifteen pounds.
What did he do on ....?
He cashed a cheque for/spent/paid in ....

Exercise A

1 Mr Perkins cashed a cheque for £15 on December 14th.
2 **Mr Perkins spent £13** ....

Drill B

Mr Perkins' balance went up on December the eighth.
Why did it go up?
Because he paid in twenty pounds.
Mr Perkins' balance went up/down on ....
Why did it go up/down?
Because he cashed a cheque for/spent/paid in ....

Exercise B

1 Mr Perkins' balance went up on December 8th because he paid in £20.
2 **Mr Perkins' balance went down on December 20th** ....

Drill C

How much money did Mr Perkins have in the bank on December the third?
Ninety-seven pounds.
How much money did he have in the bank on ....?
....

Exercise C

1 Mr Perkins had £97 in the bank on December 3rd.
2 **Mr Perkins had £48** ....

Drill D

Was there much money in Mr Perkins' account on January the fifth?
There was seventy-five pounds.
Was there much money in his account on ....?
There was ....

Exercise D

1 There was £75 in Mr Perkins' account on January 5th.
2 **There was £63** ....

Share Prices

Brown's	32½	-½
Clifford Food	38	
Eastern Foodstores	125	-1
Heathco	80	
Hepworth's	421	+3
London Sugar	66	-1
Matthews and Glover	120	-1
Morgan Groceries	21½	
National Fisheries	280	
Pilkington's	174	-4
Quickbake	139	-1
Savemart	163	+5
Scottish Biscuits	163	+1
Smith's Chocolate	80	-2
Southern Dairies	55	-5
United Stores	91	+1
Universal Stores	450	
Wilson Groceries	26	+2½

Drill A

How much do shares in Eastern Foodstores cost?
They're one twenty-five.
How much did they cost yesterday?
They were one twenty-six.

How much do shares in Morgan Groceries cost?
They're twenty-one and a half.
How much did they cost yesterday?
They were the same.

How much do shares in .... cost?
They're ....
How much did they cost yesterday?
They were ....

Exercise A

1 Shares in Eastern Foodstores cost 125p. They cost 126p yesterday.

2 Shares in Morgan Groceries ....

Drill B

I bought some shares in Hepworth's yesterday.
How much did you pay for them?
Four eighteen.
You were lucky. They cost four twenty-one today.

I sold some shares in Savemart yesterday.
How much did you get for them?
One fifty-eight.
That was silly. They're selling at one sixty-three today.

I bought/sold some shares in .... yesterday.
How much did you .... for them?
....
You were lucky/That was silly. They cost/They're selling at .... today.

Exercise B

1 I was lucky yesterday. I bought some shares in Hepworth's for 418p and they cost 421p today.

2 I did a silly thing yesterday. I sold some shares in Savemart ......

A Much-travelled Suitcase

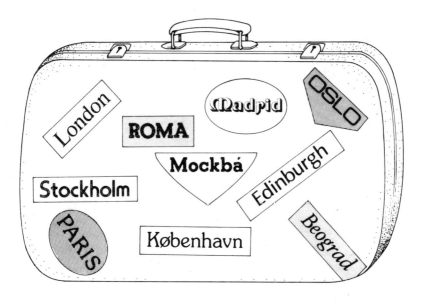

Drill A

Have you been to Barcelona?
No, but I've been to Madrid.

Have you been to ....?
No, but I've been to ....

Exercise A

1 I haven't been to Barcelona, but I've been to Madrid.
2 I haven't been to Milan ....

Drill B

I see you've been to Madrid.
Yes, have *you* ever visited Spain?
No, I haven't.

I see you've been to ....
Yes, have *you* ever visited ....?
Yes, I have/No, I haven't.

Drill C

Mr Green has just come back from Stockholm.
Yes, he's had a holiday in Sweden.

The Browns have just come back from Rome.
Yes, they've had a holiday in Italy.

.... has/have just come back from ....
Yes, he's/she's/they've had a holiday in ....

Exercise C

1 Mr Green has just come back from a holiday in Sweden.
2 The Browns ....

A Passport

Drill A

Have you been to Russia?
  Yes, I have.
When did you go there?
  In nineteen seventy-two.

Have you been to ....?
  Yes, I have.
When did you go there?
  In ....

Exercise A

1 I've been to Russia. I went there in 1972.

2 I've been to America. ....

Drill B

Where did you go on your first trip?
  I went to Norway.

Where did you go on your .... trip?
  I went to ....

Exercise B

1 My first trip was to Norway.

2 My second trip ....

Drill C

The Smiths have been to Spain, haven't they?
  Yes, but not since February seventy-one.

.... has/have been to ...., hasn't he/hasn't she/haven't they?
  Yes, but not since ....

Exercise C

1 The Smiths haven't been to Spain since February '71.

2 Mrs Robinson ....

Drill D

You've just come back from Switzerland, haven't you?
  Oh no, I came back .... years ago.

You've just come back from ...., haven't you?
  Oh no, I came back .... years ago.

Exercise D

1 I came back from Switzerland .... years ago.

2 I came back from Spain ....

Murder at the Flats

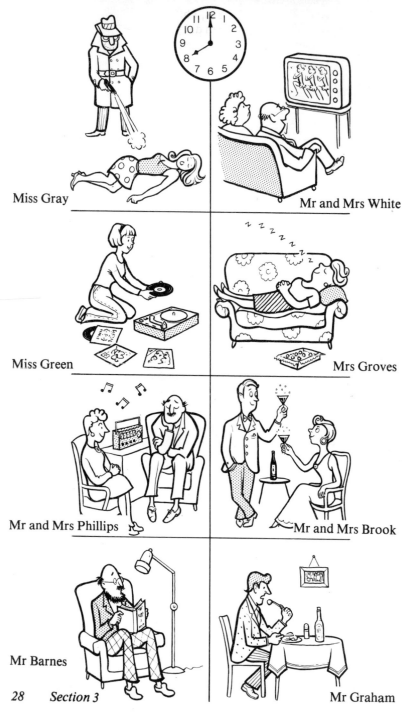

Drill A

What were you doing at eight o'clock last night, Mr Barnes?
I was reading a book.

What were you doing at eight o'clock last night, ...?
I was/We were ....

Exercise A

1 Mr Barnes was reading a book at 8 pm.

2 Mr and Mrs Phillips ....

Drill B

Did you hear the shot, Mrs Brook?
Yes, we were having a drink at the time.

Did you hear the shot, Mrs Groves?
No, I was having a nap at the time.

Did you hear the shot, ...?
Yes/No, I was/we were .... at the time.

Exercise B

1 Mr and Mrs Brook heard the shot when they were having a drink.

2 Mrs Groves didn't hear the shot because she was having a nap.

3 Mr Graham ....

Drill C

What was Mrs Groves doing when the murderer fired the shot?
She was lying on the sofa.

What was/were .... doing when the murderer fired the shot?
He was/She was/They were ....

Exercise C

1 Mrs Groves was lying on the sofa when the murderer fired the shot.

2 Mr and Mrs White ....

Olympic Medal Winners

AFTER ONE WEEK

	Gold	Silver	Bronze
1 USA	20	22	17
2 Soviet Union	18	15	11
3 East Germany	13	9	17
4 Japan	8	6	7
5 West Germany	6	7	12
6 Australia	4	5	3
7 Holland	3	2	1
8 Sweden	3	1	2
9 Bulgaria	2	5	0
10 Denmark	2	2	0
11 Britain	1	4	4
12 France	1	4	3
13 Finland	1	1	5
14 Iran	1	0	0
15 Norway	1	0	1
16 Kenya	0	1	1

AFTER TWO WEEKS

	Gold	Silver	Bronze
1 Soviet Union	56	33	17
2 USA	29	28	33
3 East Germany	24	18	25
4 Japan	12	11	7
5 West Germany	10	19	20
6 Britain	7	9	16
7 Australia	6	5	4
8 Bulgaria	4	7	5
9 Holland	4	3	1
10 Denmark	4	2	0
11 Sweden	3	4	6
12 France	2	7	6
13 Finland	2	1	3
14 Iran	2	0	2
15 Norway	2	0	1
16 Kenya	1	3	1

Drill A

Did the Soviet Union win more silver medals in the first week or in the second?
   They won more in the second week.
Did Finland win more gold medals in the first week or the second?
   They won the same number.
Did .... win more gold/silver/bronze medals in the first week or the second?
   They won ....

Exercise A

1 The Soviet Union won more silver medals in the second week than they did in the first.
2 Finland won the same number of gold medals in the second week as they did in the first.
3 France ....

Drill B

How many bronze medals did France win?
   Six.
How many had they won after the first week?
   Three.
How many gold/silver/bronze medals did .... win?
   ....
How many had they won after the first week?
   ....

Exercise B

1 France won 6 bronze medals. They had won 3 after the first week.
2 Kenya won ....

Drill C

Bulgaria were ninth after the first week, weren't they?
   Yes, but they'd gone up to eighth place by the end of the games.
.... were .... after the first week, weren't they?
   Yes, but they'd gone up/down to .... place by the end of the games.

Exercise C

1 By the end of the games Bulgaria had moved up from 9th to 8th place.
2 By the end of the games Sweden ....

FOOTBALL RESULTS

```
P = played
W = games won
D = games drawn
L = games lost
F = goals scored
A = goals against
Pts = points scored
```

LEAGUE DIVISION I

ARSENAL ...(0) 0   COVENTRY .(1) 2
33,699   Alderson, Hutchison
BIRMINGHM (0) 0   TOTTENHAM.(0) 0
38,504
CRYSTAL P..(1) 1   EVERTON ...(0) 0
Rogers   28,614
IPSWICH .....(2) 2   LEEDS ....(1) 2
Madeley (o.g.),   Charlton, Lorimer
Whymark   27,566
LEICESTER ..(0) 2   MAN. UTD. .(1) 2
Sammels,   Best, Davies
Farrington   32,575
LIVERPOOL .(1) 3   CHELSEA ....(0) 1
Toshack 2,   Baldwin 48,932
Keegan
MAN CITY ..(2) 4   DERBY ...... (0) 0
Carrodus, Marsh,   35,566
Bell, Todd (og)
SHEFF. UTD. (0) 0   STOKE ..... (0) 0
19,323
SOUTHMPTN (1) 1   NORWICH ...(0) 0
McCarthy   17,775
WEST BROM (1) 2   NEWCASTLE (1) 3
Suggett, Gould   Smith, Tudor 2
14,379
WEST HAM ..(0) 2   WOLVES ......(0) 2
Robson, Brooking   Kindon 2 29,524

LEAGUE DIVISION I

	P	W	D	L	F	A	W	D	L	F	A	Pts
				HOME						AWAY		
Liverpool	16	8	0	0	22	6	2	4	2	10	10	24
Leeds United	16	5	2	1	18	7	3	3	2	12	12	21
Arsenal	17	6	3	1	13	5	2	2	3	8	9	21
Chelsea	16	4	1	2	14	8	3	4	2	12	11	19
Tottenham Hotspur	16	5	1	1	11	6	3	2	4	12	11	19
West Ham United	16	6	2	0	23	7	1	2	5	9	14	18
Everton	16	4	2	2	11	7	3	2	3	7	7	18
Ipswich Town	16	3	3	2	12	9	3	3	2	11	11	18
Newcastle United	16	5	1	2	14	10	3	1	4	13	14	18
Norwich City	16	4	4	0	11	6	3	0	5	7	15	18
Wolverhampton Wdrs.	16	5	1	1	17	10	1	4	4	11	17	17
Southampton	16	4	3	1	10	6	1	3	4	4	8	16
Sheffield United	16	4	2	3	8	7	2	2	3	9	14	16
Coventry City	16	2	3	3	8	12	3	2	3	6	5	15
Manchester City	16	6	1	1	17	7	0	1	7	5	18	14
Derby County	16	6	0	1	11	6	0	2	7	3	20	14
Stoke City	16	4	3	0	15	6	0	1	8	8	20	12
West Bromwich Albion	16	3	3	3	10	11	1	1	5	6	11	12
Birmingham City	17	4	1	4	14	10	0	2	7	4	15	12
Leicester City	16	2	4	3	10	11	1	1	5	7	13	11
Crystal Palace	16	3	2	4	7	10	0	3	4	4	13	11
Manchester United	16	2	3	3	7	8	0	3	5	7	15	10

Drill A

Which team has won the most home games?
Liverpool.
Which team has scored the most away goals?
Newcastle United.
Which team has .... the most/fewest ....?
....

Exercise A

1 Liverpool have won the most home games.
2 Newcastle United have scored ....

Drill B

How many away games have Chelsea lost?
Two.
How many had they lost before yesterday?
One.
How many home games have Ipswich drawn?
Three.
How many had they drawn before yesterday?
Two.
How many .... games have ....?
....
How many had they .... before yesterday?
....

Exercise B

1 Before yesterday Chelsea had lost one away game. Now they have lost two.
2 Before yesterday Ipswich had drawn two home games. ....

EVENING CLASSES IN COOKERY

Cookery Attendance Register
Spring Term

Month	January					February				March				April			
Name	3	10	17	24	31	7	14	21	28	7	14	21	28	4	11	18	25
Mrs Jones	✓	✓	✓	✗	✓	✓	✓	✓	✓	✗	✓	✓	✗	✓	✓	✓	✓
Miss Baker	✓	✓	✓	✓	✓	✓	✗	✓	✓	✓	✓	✓	✓	✓	✓	✓	✓
Miss Lane	✓	✓	✗	✓	✓	✓	✓	✓	✗	✓	✓	✓	✓	✓	✓	✓	✓
Miss Dawson	—	✓	✓	✓	✓	✓	✗	✗	✓	✓	✓	✓	✗	✗	✓	✓	✓
Mrs Bell	—		✓	✓	✗	✓	✗	✓	✓	✓	✗	✓	✓	✓	✗	✓	✗
Miss Lee	—		✓	✓	✓	✓	✓	✓	✓	✗	✓	✓	✓	✓	✓	✓	✓
Mrs Grey	—					✓	✗	✓	✗	✓	✗	✓	✗	✓	✗	✓	✗	✓
Miss Roberts	—						✓	✓	✓	✓	✓	✓	✗	✗	✓	✓	✓
Miss Smith	—						✓	✓	✓	✗	✓	✓	✓	✗	✗	✓
Miss Jackson	—							✓	✓	✓	✓	✗	✗	✓	✓	✓
Mrs Barry	—									✓	✓	✓	✓	✓	✓	✗
Mrs Mason	—													✓	✓	✗	✓	✓

34   Section 3

Drill A

Miss Roberts takes cookery lessons, doesn't she?
  Yes, she's been coming since the fourteenth of February.

.... takes cookery lessons, doesn't she?
  Yes, she's been coming since the .... of ....

Exercise A

1 Miss Roberts has been taking cookery lessons since Feb. 14th.

2 Mrs Jones ....

Drill B

How long has Miss Baker been learning cookery?
  For seventeen weeks.

How long has .... been learning cookery?
  For .... weeks.

Exercise B

1 Miss Baker has been learning cookery for 17 weeks.

2 Miss Mason ....

Drill C

How many times has Mrs Jones been absent this term?
  Three times.

How many times has Miss Baker been absent this term?
  Once.

How many times has .... been absent this term?
  ....

Exercise C

1 Mrs Jones has been absent three times this term.

2 Miss Baker ....

DON'T FORGET

Mon   Buy birthday present

Tue   Meet Susie

Wed   Have driving lesson

Thu   Go to dentist

Fri   See bank manager

Sat   Do shopping

Sun   Visit parents

Drill A

What are you going to do on Monday?
 Buy a birthday present.

What are you going to do on............?
 ....

Exercise A

1 I'm going to buy a birthday present on Monday.

2 I'm going to ....

Drill B

Are you doing anything on Wednesday?
 Yes, I'm having a driving lesson.

Are you doing anything on ....?
 Yes, I'm ....

Exercise B

1 I'm having a driving lesson on Wednesday.

2 I'm ....

Drill C

Will you have time to see me on Thursday afternoon?
 I'm afraid not. I'll be going to the dentist.

Will you have time to see me on .... afternoon?
 I'm afraid not. I'll be ....

Exercise C

1 I'll be going to the dentist on Thursday afternoon.

2 I'll be visiting ....

Drill D

I'm going to repair my car on Friday.
 Well, I'll come and help you when I've seen my bank manager.

I'm going to paint the living room on Tuesday.
 Well, I'll come and help you when I've met Susie.

I'm going to .... on ....
 Well, I'll come and help you when I've ....

Royal Festival Hall

Sun 3 Oct 3.15 pm.	Royal Philharmonic Orchestra	Bach - Brandenburg 　　Concerto No. 2 Ravel - Bolero
Sun 3 Oct 7.30 pm.	B.B.C. Symphony Orchestra	Liszt - Piano Concerto 　　No. 2 Beethoven - Symphony 　　No. 7
Mon 4 Oct 8 pm.	Chicago Symphony Orchestra	Dvorak - Slavonic 　　Dances Bartok - Concerto for 　　Orchestra
Tues 5 Oct 8 pm.	New Philharmonia Orchestra	Mendelssohn - Overture to A Midsummer Night's Dream Mozart - Symphony 　　No. 34
Wed 6 Oct 8 pm.	Scottish National Orchestra	Ravel - Rapsodie Espagnol Chopin - Piano Concerto 　　No. 1
Thurs 7 Oct 8 pm.	B.B.C. Symphony Orchestra	Tchaikovsky - Symphony 　　No. 4 Stravinsky - The Firebird
Fri 8 Oct 8 pm.	Chicago Symphony Orchestra	Mozart - Piano Concerto 　　No. 21 Sibelius - Symphony 　　No. 5
Sat 9 Oct 8 pm.	Royal Philharmonic Orchestra	Handel - Water Music Beethoven - Symphony 　　No. 5

Drill A

What's on at the Royal Festival Hall on Sunday afternoon?
  The Royal Philharmonic Orchestra are giving a concert of Bach and Ravel.

What's on at the Royal Festival Hall on ....?
  The .... are giving a concert of .... and ....

Exercise A

1 The Royal Philharmonic Orchestra are giving a concert of Bach and Ravel at the Royal Festival Hall on Sunday afternoon.

2 The Chicago Symphony Orchestra ....

Drill B

Which of Liszt's works is being performed on Sunday evening?
  The piano concerto number two.

Which of ....'s works is being performed on ....?
  The ....

Exercise B

1 Liszt's piano concerto no. 2 is being performed on Sunday evening.

2 Mozart's symphony no. 34 ....

Drill C

Are you going to buy tickets for the concert on Wednesday?
  Yes, I'd like to hear the Scottish National Orchestra. They're playing Ravel and Chopin.

Are you going to buy tickets for the concert on ....?
  Yes, I'd like to hear the .... They're playing ....

Exercise C

1 I'm going to buy tickets for the concert on Wednesday when the Scottish National Orchestra are playing Ravel and Chopin.

2 I'm going to buy tickets for the concert on Friday ....

HOLIDAYS

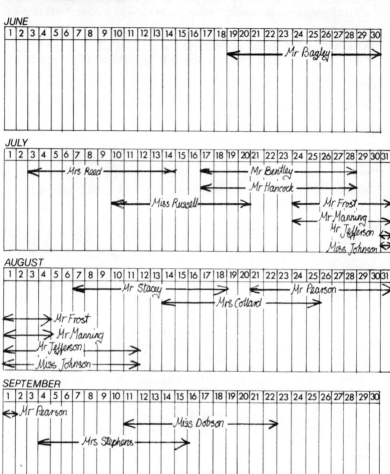

Drill A

When is Mr Manning taking his holiday?
From July the twenty-fourth to August the fourth.

When is ………… taking his/her holiday?
From ………… the ………… to ………… the ………….

Exercise A

1 Mr Manning is taking his holiday from July 24th to August 4th.
2 Mrs Collard ………….

Drill B

Will Mr Stacey be working on July the eighteenth?
Yes, he will.

Will Mr Pearson be working on August the twenty-third?
No, he won't.

Will ………… be working on …………?
Yes/No, he/she will/won't.

Exercise B

1 Mr Stacey will be working on July 18th.
2 Mr Pearson ………….

Drill C

Can I make an appointment to see Mrs Collard on August the sixteenth?
I'm afraid not . She won't be back from her holiday till the **twenty-sixth.**

Can I make an appointment to see ………… on …………?
I'm afraid not. He/She won't be back from his/her holiday till the ………….

Exercise C

1 Mrs Collard won't be back from her holiday until August 25th.
2 Miss Russell ………….

Puriton Cricket Club
FIXTURES

April	22	East Huntspill	Won
	29	Bason Bridge	Drawn
May	6	Enmore	Drawn
	13	Ashcott	Won
	20	Mark	Drawn
	27	Chilton Polden	Won
June	3	North Newton	Lost
	10	Kilve	Lost
	17	West Huntspill	Won
	24	Wedmore	
July	1	Cannington	
	8	Shapwick	
	15	Nether Stowey	
	22	North Curry	
	29	North Petherton	
August	5	Spaxton	
	12	Brent Knoll	

Drill A

Have your team played Enmore yet?
    Yes, we played them on May the sixth.

Have you played Cannington yet?
    No, we're playing them on July the first.

Have you played .... yet?
    ....

Exercise A

1 Puriton played Enmore on May 6th.

2 They're playing Cannington ....

Drill B

How did your team do against East Huntspill?
    We beat them.

How did you do against Kilve?
    We lost to them.

How did you do against Enmore?
    We drew with them.

How did you do against Shapwick?
    We haven't played them yet.

How did you do against ....?
    ....

Exercise B

1 Puriton beat East Huntspill.

2 They haven't played ....

ADDRESSES

John & Mary Green
41 Southampton Rd
London

3 Middleton Crescent
Dover

Leslie Pattersen
19 Lexden Gardens
Edinburgh

27 Madison Park
Toronto

Mark & Betty Davidson
6 Park Crescent
Glasgow

4 Livingstone Rd
London

Kay Simpson
24 Cherry Grove
Manchester

2 Landseer Avenue
Leeds

Tom & Dorothy Browning
10 Byron Place
Bristol

29 Independence Avenue
Lagos

Jim Moore
15 High St
Colchester

33 Seaview Drive
Folkestone

Fred & Louise Roberts
58 Hampstead Rd
London

2 MacDonald St
Aberdeen

George & Elizabeth Dobson
133 Fairbanks Lane
Cheltenham

17 Barnes St
Batley

Drill A

Where did the Greens used to live?
 At forty-one Southampton Road, London.
Where do they live now?
 At three Middleton Crescent, Dover.

Where did .... used to live?
 At ....
Where .... live now?
 At ....

Exercise A

1 The Greens used to live in London but now they live in Dover.

2 Jim Moore ....

Drill B

Do Fred and Louise still live in London?
 No, they've moved. They live in Aberdeen now.
Does/Do .... still live in ....?
 No, ... moved. .... live in .... now.

Exercise B

1 Fred and Louise don't live in London any more. They've moved to Aberdeen.

2 Jim ....

Drill C

Jim lives in Colchester, doesn't he?
 No, he's moved to Folkestone.

.... lives /live in ...., doesn't/don't he/she/they?
 No, ... moved to ....

Section 5

Hotel Bookings
at 8-2-76

The Piccadilly Palace Hotel

ROOM	NAME	BOOKED FROM	UP TO
22	Mr & Mrs Percy	31.1.76	5.2.76
45	Miss Jacklin	1.2.76	3.2.76
16	Mr Fraser	1.2.76	6.2.76
33	Mr & Mrs Livingstone	2.2.76	3.2.76
25	Mr Wilson	3.2.76	7.2.76
56	Mr & Mrs Fairfax	4.2.76	9.2.76
20	Mr Johnson	4.2.76	18.2.76
32	Miss Davis	4.2.76	10.2.76
22	Mr & Mrs Leslie	5.2.76	12.2.76
41	Mrs Morton	6.2.76	16.2.76
35	Mr Bell	6.2.76	6.3.76
27	Mr & Mrs Dixon	6.2.76	16.2.76
29	Mr & Mrs Graham	6.2.76	10.2.76
31	Mr & Mrs Smith	7.2.76	14.2.76
43	Mr Green	7.2.76	21.2.76
26	Miss Grant	8.2.76	11.2.76

Section 5

Drill A

How long have the Fairfaxes been staying here?
   Since the fourth.

How long has/have .... been staying here?
   Since the ....

Exercise A

1 The Fairfaxes have been staying here since the 4th.
2 Mr Fraser ....

Drill B

Will Mrs Morton be leaving today?
   No, she won't be leaving until the sixteenth.

Will .... be leaving today?
   No, ./.......... won't be leaving until the............

Exercise B

1 Mrs Morton won't be leaving until the 16th.
2 Mr and Mrs Graham ....

Drill C

Will room twenty-two be free on the fifteenth of February?
   Yes. Mr and Mrs Leslie will have left by then.

Will room .... be free on the .... of ....?
   Yes/No. .... will/won't have left by then.

Exercise C

1 Mr and Mrs Leslie will have left by 15th Feb.
2 Mr Johnson ....

Drill D

Are the Livingstones still here?
   No, they've already left. They went five days ago.

Is Mr Green still here?
   Yes, he hasn't left yet. He'll be here for another thirteen days.

Is/Are .... still here?
   ....

Exercise D

1 The Livingstones aren't here any longer. They left 5 days ago.
2 Mr Green is still here ....

A Sale

Drill A

How much is that dress?
It was twelve pounds before, but now it's only ten pounds.

How much is that/are those ....?
It was/They were .... before, but now it's/they're only ....

Exercise A

1 That dress was £12 before, but now it's only £10.

2 Those shoes ....

Drill B

Look at that raincoat! That's a bargain.
Yes, they were charging fifteen pounds for it last week, but now it's going for eleven pounds fifty.

Look at that/those ....! That's a bargain.
Yes, they were charging .... for it/them last week, but now it's/they're going for ....

Exercise B

1 They were charging £15 for that raincoat last week, but now it's going for £11.50.

2 They were charging ....

Drill C

What a pity you bought that shirt last week!
Yes, I wish I'd waited until the sale. I've wasted two pounds fifty.

What a pity you bought that/those .... last week!
Yes, I wish I'd waited until the sale. I've wasted ....

Exercise C

1 I wish I had waited until the sale to buy that shirt. I've wasted £2.50.

2 I wish I had waited until the sale to buy some ....

Section 5

A One-way System

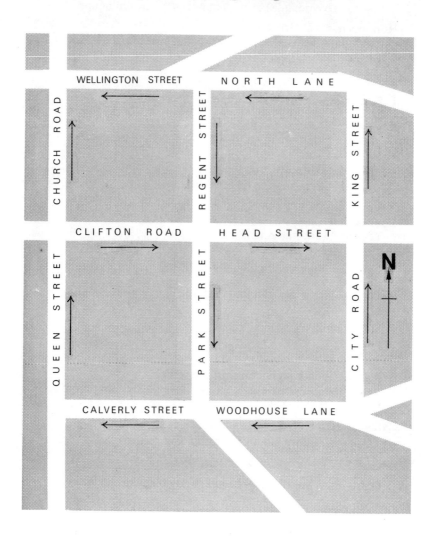

Drill A

Which way do you have to go along Park Street?
You have to go south.
Which way do you have to go along ....?
You have to go ....

Exercise A

1 You have to go south along Park St.
2 You have to ....

Drill B

Can you go east along Head Street?
Yes, you can.
Can you go south along King Street?
No, you can't, you have to go north.
Can you go .... along ....?
....

Exercise B

1 You can go east along Head St.
2 You ....

Drill C

Let's go along King Street and into Head Street.
But you aren't allowed to go south along King Street. You'll have to go another way.
Let's go along .... and into ....
But you aren't allowed to go .... along .... You'll have to go another way.

Exercise C

1 You aren't allowed to go south along King St.; you have to go another way.
2 You aren't allowed to go ....

Section 6

A SLIMMING DIET

On waking	Cup of tea
Breakfast	Egg Slice of bread and butter Cup of tea
10.30 a.m.	Cup of tea
Lunch	3 ounces of meat Green vegetables Fruit Cup of tea
4.00 p.m.	Slice of bread and butter Cup of tea
Evening	2 ounces of meat Green vegetables Small banana Cup of tea
Bedtime	Glass of milk

To be avoided:

potatoes	biscuits
rice	cake
sugar	sweets
jam	alcohol

Drill A

Can you have meat on your diet?
   Yes, I can.

Can you have potatoes?
   No, I mustn't.

Can you have ....?
   ....

Exercise A

1 I can have meat, but I mustn't have potatoes.

2 I can have ....

Drill B

Can't I have a piece of bread with my morning tea?
   Well, you oughtn't to, you know.

Can't I have some biscuits at bedtime?
   Well, you oughtn't to, you know.

Can't I have a/some ....?
   Well, you oughtn't to, you know.

Exercise B

1 The doctor says I oughtn't to have a piece of bread with my morning tea.

2 The doctor says I oughtn't to have any biscuits.

3 The doctor says ....

Drill C

Would you like some chips?
   I'd love some but I'm on a diet. Could I have some peas instead?

Would you like ....?
   I'd love one/some but I'm on a diet. Could I have .... instead?

Section 6

ROAD SIGNS 1

1

Horses or ponies

2

Trains

3

Children

4

Cattle

5

Wild animals

6

Pedestrians

7

Workmen

8

Fallen rocks

Drill A

Look at number five. Why should you be careful?
There may be wild animals on the road.

Look at number .... Why should you be careful?
There may be .... on/crossing the road.

Exercise A

1 Be careful! There may be horses or ponies on the road.

2 Be careful! There may be ....

Drill B

Look at number two. Why ought you to drive carefully when you see this sign?
In case there are any trains crossing the road.

Look at number .... Why ought you to drive carefully when you see this sign?
In case there are any .... on/crossing the road.

Exercise B

1 Drive carefully in case there are any horses or ponies on the road.

2 Drive carefully ....

Drill C

Look at number four. What might happen if a driver didn't pay attention to this sign?
He might run over a cow.

Look at number .... What might happen if a driver didn't pay attention to this sign?
He might run over/into a ....

Exercise C

1 If a driver didn't pay attention to this sign, he might run over a horse.

2 If a driver ....

Drill D

Look at number seven. Don't you have to stop?
No, you don't have to unless there are workmen on the road.

Look at number .... Don't you have to stop?
No, you don't have to/needn't unless there are .... on/crossing the road.

Exercise D

1 You needn't stop unless there are horses or ponies on the road.

2 You needn't stop ....

ROAD SIGNS 2

1

Maximum speed

2

No walking

3

Minimum speed

4

No stopping

5

No entry

6

No cycling

7

No overtaking

8

No right turn

9

No left turn

10

No U turns

Section 6

Drill A

Look at number one. What mustn't you do when you see this sign?
You mustn't go at more than thirty miles an hour.

Look at number .... What mustn't you do when you see this sign?
You mustn't ....

Exercise A

1 You mustn't go at more than 30 mph.

2 You mustn't ....

Drill B

Look at number seven. What aren't you allowed to do when you see this sign?
You aren't allowed to overtake.

Look at number .... What aren't you allowed to do when you see this sign?
You aren't allowed to ....

Exercise B

1 You aren't allowed to go at more than 30 mph.

2 You aren't allowed ....

Drill C

I'm going to turn right here.
But the sign says you're not to turn right.

I'm going to .... here.
But the sign says you're not to ....

Exercise C

1 This sign says that you are not to drive at more than 30 mph.

2 This sign ....

Section 6   57

ROAD SIGNS 3

1
Cross roads

2
Roundabout

3
T junction

4
Steep hill

5
Traffic lights

6
Hump bridge

7
Series of bends

8
Level crossing

9
Uneven road

Drill A

Look at number six. Why must you slow down?
  Because there's a hump bridge ahead.

Look at number .... Why must you slow down?
  Because there is/are .... ahead.

Exercise A

1 You must slow down because there are cross roads ahead.

2 You must ....

Drill B

Am I driving too fast?
  Yes. You'd better drive more slowly. We're coming to a T-junction.

Am I driving too fast?
  Yes. You'd better drive more slowly. We're coming to ....

Exercise B

1 You ought to drive more carefully when approaching cross roads.

2 You ought to ....

Drill C

You shouldn't drive so fast: there are traffic lights ahead.

You shouldn't/oughtn't to drive so fast: there is/are .... ahead.

Exercise C

1 You should drive more slowly because of the series of bends ahead.

2 You ought to ....

London Theatres

THEATRES

ADELPHI   836 7611   Evenings 7.30.
SALLY ANN HOWES
and PETER WYNGARDE in
RODGERS & HAMMERSTEIN'S
THE KING AND I

ALBERY   836 3878   Evenings 8.0.
INGRID BERGMAN and JOHN McCALLUM
THE CONSTANT WIFE
by Somerset Maugham
Directed by John Gielgud

ALDWYCH   836 6404
SECTION NINE
by Philip Magdalany
(Evenings 7.30.   Sat. 2.30. & 7.30.)

AMBASSADORS   836 1171
Evenings 8.0. Matinees Tues. 2.45 & Sat. 5.0.
AGATHA CHRISTIE'S
THE MOUSETRAP

ROYAL COURT   730 1745
Directed by Athol Fugard
STATEMENTS
Evenings 7.30.

ST. MARTIN'S   836 1443   Evenings 8.0.
Matinees wed. 2.45. & Sat. 5.0.
IRENE HANDL, ROY KINNEAR
and AIMI MacDONALD in
DEAD EASY
A new comedy by Jack Popplewell

SAVOY   836 8888   Evenings 8.0.
JOHN MILLS in
William Douglas Home's
AT THE END OF THE DAY

HAYMARKET   930 9832   Evenings 8.0.
Matinee Wed. 2.30.
PHYLLIS CALVERT, JOHN FRASER,
and ANDREW RAY in
CROWN MATRIMONIAL

GREENWICH   858 7755   Evenings   8.0.
Matinee Sat. 2.30.
GHOSTS
BY IBSEN

GLOBE   437 1592   Evenings   8.15.
Sat. 5.40 & 8.40.
JILL BENNETT and JOHN STANDING in
NOEL COWARD'S
PRIVATE LIVES
Directed by John Gielgud

GARRICK   856 4001   Evenings   8.0.
Sat. 5.30 & 8.30.
DANDY DICK

OLD VIC   928 7616   Evenings   7.30.
THE PARTY

NEW LONDON THEATRE   405 0072
Evenings   8.0.   Sat.   5.30.   &   8.30.
THE SMASH HIT
ROCK'N ROLL MUSICAL
GREASE

MAYFAIR   629 3036   Evenings 8.15.
ROY DOTRICE in
BRIEF LIVES

MERMAID   248 7656   Evenings 7.30.
Sat.   5.45. & 8.30.
A NEW MUSICAL
TREASURE ISLAND

LYRIC   437 1592   Evenings 8.0.
Matinees   Wed.   3.0.   &   Sat.   6.0.
ALEC GUINNESS in
HABEAS CORPUS
By Alan Bennett

Drill A

Let's go to *The King and I*, shall we?
Yes, let's. Will you phone the Adelphi and book the tickets?

Let's go to ...., shall we?
Yes, let's. Will you phone the .... and book the tickets?

Exercise A

1 Will you phone the Adelphi and book tickets for *The King and I*?
2 Will you phone the Greenwich ....?

Drill B

Treasure Island is on at the Mermaid. Shall we go?
Oh, I've seen it. Could we go to *Dandy Dick* instead?

.... is on at the .... Shall we go?
Oh, I've seen it. Could we go to .... instead?

Exercise B

1 Could we go to *Dandy Dick* instead of *Treasure Island*?
2 Could we go to *Private Lives* ....

Drill C

I've got to pick up our tickets for *Section Nine* today.
I'll be passing the Aldwych this afternoon. I'll get them for you, shall I?

I've got to pick up our tickets for .... today.
I'll be passing the .... this afternoon. I'll get them for you, shall I?

Exercise C

1 I'll pick up our tickets for *Section Nine* when I'm passing the Aldwych.
2 I'll ....

ROAD ACCIDENTS IN WESTSHIRE

	Deaths			Injuries		
	Pedestrians	Cyclists	Drivers	Pedestrians	Cyclists	Drivers
Jan	1 (0)	0 (0)	1 (1)	2 (2)	2 (2)	6 (3)
Feb	1 (2)	1 (0)	2 (2)	3 (3)	2 (2)	7 (4)
Mar	0 (0)	0 (2)	0 (0)	4 (1)	2 (1)	0 (2)
Apr	1 (0)	0 (1)	1 (1)	2 (1)	1 (4)	4 (1)
May	1 (0)	2 (0)	1 (0)	4 (1)	2 (4)	9 (6)
Jun	0 (0)	0 (0)	0 (2)	3 (1)	0 (2)	2 (2)
Jul	1 (0)	0 (1)	3 (0)	4 (3)	1 (3)	4 (3)
Aug	2 (1)	1 (2)	3 (1)	4 (6)	2 (3)	10 (8)
Sep	0 (0)	0 (0)	2 (0)	0 (2)	0 (3)	5 (3)
Oct	1 (0)	1 (1)	2 (2)	2 (3)	1 (4)	12 (8)
Nov	0 (0)	0 (0)	0 (0)	4 (2)	2 (2)	1 (3)
Dec	(0)	(0)	(1)	(5)	(3)	(6)
	8 (3)	5 (7)	15 (10)	32 (30)	15 (33)	60 (49)

(Last year's totals in brackets)

Drill A

Were there a lot of injuries to pedestrians in June this year?
   Three pedestrians were injured.

Were there a lot of deaths among drivers in April last year?
   One driver was killed.

Were there a lot of injuries/deaths .... in .... this/last year?
   ....

Exercise A

1 Three pedestrians were injured in June this year.

2 One driver ....

Drill B

Five cyclists have been killed so far this year.
   Seven were killed last year.

.... have been killed/injured so far this year.
.... were killed/injured last year.

Exercise B

1 5 cyclists have been killed so far this year whereas 7 were killed last year.

2 32 pedestrians ....

Drill C

Sixty drivers have been injured so far this year.
   Far too many drivers are getting injured on our roads.

.... have been/were .... so far this year/last year.
   Far too many .... are getting .... on our roads.

Exercise C

1 Far too many drivers are getting injured on our roads. 60 have been injured so far this year.

2 Far too many cyclists are ....

A Reading List

Joseph Conrad - *Nostromo* (1905), Dent
E. M. Forster - *A Passage to India* (1924), Arnold
John Steinbeck - *Grapes of Wrath* (1939), Viking Press
Henry Miller - *Tropic of Capricorn* (1939), Panther
George Orwell - *Animal Farm* (1945), Secker and Warburg
Kingsley Amis - *Lucky Jim* (1954), Gollancz
Graham Greene - *The Quiet American* (1955), Heinemann
John Braine - *Room at the Top* (1957), Eyre and Spottiswoode
Alan Sillitoe - *Saturday Night and Sunday Morning* (1958), Pan
Iris Murdoch - *The Bell* (1958), Chatto and Windus
Stan Barstow *A Kind of Loving* (1960), Joseph
Joseph Heller - *Catch 22* (1961), Corgi
B.S. Johnson - *Travelling People* (1963), Constable
Len Deighton - *Funeral in Berlin* (1964), Cape

Drill A

When was *Room at the Top* first published?
　In nineteen fifty-seven.

When was .... first published?
　In ....

Exercise A

1 *Room at the Top* was first published in 1957.

2 *A Passage to India* ....

Drill B

Who wrote *The Quiet American*?
　It was written by Graham Greene.
And who publishes it?
　It's published by Heinemann.

Who wrote ....?
　It was written by ....
And who publishes it?
　It's published by ....

Exercise B

1 *The Quiet American* was written by Graham Greene and is published by Heinemann.

2 *Animal Farm* ....

Drill C

I see John Steinbeck has been put on your reading list.
　Yes, we'll be expected to read *Grapes of Wrath*.

I see .... has been put on your reading list.
　Yes, we'll be expected to read ....

Exercise C

1 We'll be expected to read *Grapes of Wrath* by John Steinbeck which has been put on our reading list.

2 We'll be expected to read *The Bell* ....

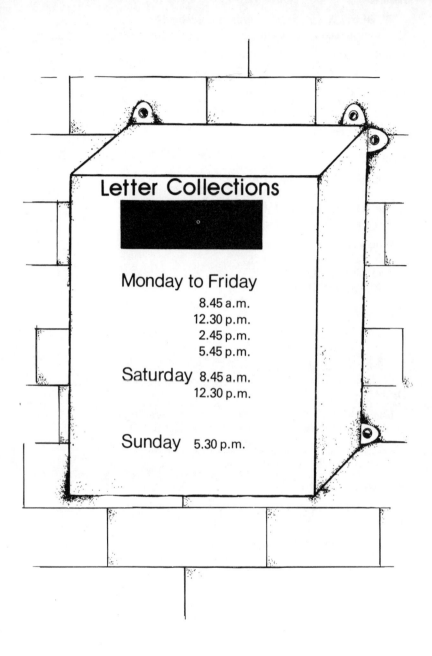

Drill A

I'll post this letter about three on Friday afternoon.
Well, it won't go until quarter to six if you leave it till three in the afternoon.

I'll post this letter about .... on .... morning/afternoon/evening.
Well, it won't go until .... if you leave it till .... in the ....

Exercise A

1 If you post the letter on Friday afternoon, it will go at 5.45 p.m.
2 If you post the letter on Wednesday morning, ...

Drill B

If I posted a letter at four o'clock on Saturday afternoon, when would it be collected?
At half past five on Sunday afternoon.

If I posted a letter at .... on ...., when would it be collected?
At ....

Exercise B

1 If I posted a letter at 4.00 p.m. on Saturday, it would be collected at 5.30 p.m. on Sunday.

2 If I posted a letter at 10.00 a.m. on Monday, ...

Drill C

I posted that letter at nine o'clock on Tuesday morning.
If you had posted it a bit earlier, you would have caught the first post.

I posted that letter at .... on ....
If you had posted it a bit earlier, you would have caught the .... post.

Exercise C

1 If you had posted the letter at 8.45 a.m. instead of 9.00 a.m., you would have caught the first post.

2 If you had posted the letter at 12.30 p.m. ....

A SAVINGS SCHEME

AMOUNT SAVED EACH MONTH	SAVINGS AFTER 5 YEARS	BONUS AFTER 5 YEARS
£1	£60	£12
2	120	24
3	180	36
4	240	48
5	300	60
6	360	72
7	420	84
8	480	96
9	540	108
10	600	120
11	660	132
12	720	144
13	780	156
14	840	168
15	900	180
16	960	192
17	1,020	204
18	1,080	216
19	1,140	228
20	1,200	240

Drill A
If I save one pound a month, how much will I have saved after five years?
   Sixty pounds.
If I save .... a month, how much will I have saved after five years?
   ....

Exercise A
1 If I save £1 a month, I will have saved £60 after 5 years.
2 If I save £8 a month ....

Drill B
I save five pounds every month.
   If you go on doing that, you'll get a bonus of sixty pounds after five years.
I save .... pounds every month.
   If you go on doing that, you'll get a bonus of .... after five years.

Exercise B
1 If you save £5 every month, you will get a bonus of £60 in 5 years time.
2 If you save £10 ....

Drill C
I wish I could put fifteen pounds into a savings scheme every month.
   If you did, you'd receive a bonus of a hundred and eighty pounds after five years.
I wish I could put .... into a savings scheme every month.
   If you did, you'd receive a bonus of .... after five years.

Exercise C
1 If I put £15 into a savings scheme every month, I would receive a bonus of £180 after 5 years.
2 If I put £10 ....

Drill D
I started to save six pounds a month five years ago but I couldn't keep it up.
   What a pity! If you had kept it up, you'd have had a bonus of seventy-two pounds now.
I started to save .... a month five years ago but I couldn't keep it up.
   What a pity! If you had kept it up, you'd have had a bonus of .... now.

Exercise D
1 If I had saved £6 a month for the last 5 years, I would have had a bonus of £72 now.
2 If I had saved £2 ....

YOUR HOROSCOPE

Your family will give you a pleasant surprise this week. Don't be careless with money. You should save more.

Your business affairs will turn out better than you expected. Don't be too friendly to strangers. You should spend more time at home.

A letter will make you change your mind. Don't go on any journeys. You should take up new interests.

You will have some problems with your work. Don't worry too much. You should enjoy life more.

Your friends will disappoint you. Don't change any of your plans. You should go out more and meet new people.

An old friend you haven't seen for years will visit you. Don't tell any secrets. You should try to take a holiday.

An important meeting will take place between you and your boss. Don't lose your temper. You should try to find a new job.

You will have a quarrel with someone you love. Don't leave home. You should pay more attention to your friends.

You will receive an unexpected invitation from one of your friends. Don't accept any invitations. You should do more work.

You will meet an interesting stranger through your job. Don't make any decisions this weekend. You should think carefully about your future.

You will soon be able to earn more money. Don't do anything dangerous. You should start making plans for next year.

You will have to visit someone who lives very far away. Don't go on a journey alone. You should ask your friends to help you.

Drill A

Do you believe in horoscopes?
    Yes, my horoscope last week said my family would give me a pleasant surprise, and they did.

Do you believe in horoscopes?
    No, my horoscope last week said I would have some problems with my work, and I didn't.

Do you believe in horoscopes?
    Yes/No, my horoscope last week said .... would ...., and .... did/didn't.

Exercise A *(Write down what your horoscope said last week)*

My horoscope last week ....

Drill B

What warning are Aries people given?
    Not to change any of their plans.

What warning are .... people given?
    Not to ....

Exercise B

1 Aries people are warned not to change any of their plans.

2 Cancer ....

Drill C

I'm Cancer. What advice does the horoscope give me this week?
    To start making plans for next year.

I'm .... What advice does the horoscope give me this week?
    To ....

Exercise C

1 Cancer people are advised to start making plans for next year.

2 Leo ....

SUGGESTIONS BOOK
The Metropolitan Hotel

The management welcomes suggestions from hotel guests. Please write any complaints here.

You ought to serve lunch until 2.30. The dining-room is too crowded — Mrs Joseph.

It might be a good idea to turn the heating on earlier. The bedrooms are cold — Mr. Mills.

Why don't you close the discotheque at midnight? The noise of music keeps guests awake — Mrs Duncan.

Have you thought of putting telephones in the bedrooms? Guests can't make phone calls — Mr Castle.

You should offer a wider choice of food. Guests get tired of the menu. Mrs. Patterson.

Couldn't you improve the hot water supply? Guests can't get enough hot water in the evening — Miss Jones.

How about enlarging the car park? Some guests have to leave their cars out on the road — Mr. Davis.

You could provide more towels. Guests who go swimming don't have enough towels — Miss White.

Have you thought of building a swimming pool? The beach is too far away. Mr. Thomson.

I think you should reduce your prices. The hotel costs too much — Mr. Grant.

Drill A

Had Mrs Joseph any suggestion to make?
  Yes, she suggested they should serve lunch until two thirty.

Had .... any suggestion to make?
  Yes, he/she suggested they should ....

Exercise A

1 Mrs Joseph suggested (that) they should serve lunch until 2.30.
2 Mr Davis ....

Drill B

Had Mr Castle any complaint to make?
  Yes, he complained that guests couldn't make phone calls.

Had .... any complaint to make?
  Yes, he/she complained that ....

Exercise B

1 Mr Castle complained that guests couldn't make phone calls.
2 Miss White ....

Drill C

Did Mr Thomson enjoy his stay at the hotel?
  Well, he thought they should build a swimming pool because the beach was too far away.

Did .... enjoy his/her stay at the hotel?
  Well, he/she thought that they should .... because ....

Exercise C

1 Mr Thomson thought they should build a swimming pool because the beach was too far away.
2 Mrs Duncan ....

Leisure Activities

	% doing the activity at least once a month
Home activities	
Watching television	97
Gardening	64
Playing with children	62
Decorating	53
Cleaning the car	48
Sporting activities	
Swimming	22
Fishing	8
Table tennis	6
Sailing	2
Other activities	
Going for a drive	58
Going to a pub	52
Going for a walk	47
Eating out	32

Drill A

Going to the pub is a popular activity.
  Gardening is even more popular.

.... is a popular activity.
  .... is even more popular.

Exercise A

1 Gardening is a more popular activity than going to the pub.

2 Decorating ....

Drill B

Do you like going for a drive?
  Yes, and I enjoy going for a walk too.

Do you like swimming?
  No, I prefer fishing.

Do you like ....?
  Yes, and I enjoy .... too./No, I prefer ....

Exercise B

1 I enjoy going for a walk as well as going for a drive.

2 I prefer fishing to swimming.

3 I ....

Drill C

Would you like to eat out?
  Well, I was hoping to watch television.

Would you like to ....?
  Well, I was hoping to ....

Exercise C

1 I don't want to eat out; I was hoping to watch television.

2 I don't want to ....

Section 7

A Vegetable Garden

Jan	Plan vegetable garden
Feb	Put fertilizer on garden
Mar	Prepare seed bed. Plant potatoes
Apr	Sow carrots and peas
May	Sow beans
Jun	Plant cabbages and celery
Jul	Lift potatoes
Aug	Water vegetables
Sep	Sow lettuce
Oct	Lift carrots
Nov	Dig garden
Dec	Lift celery

Drill A

What's the best time for sowing carrots?
  April.

What's the best time for ....?
  ....

Exercise A

1 April is the best time for sowing carrots.

2 November ....

Drill B

When are potatoes supposed to be planted?
  In March.

When is/are .... supposed to be ....?
  In ....

Exercise B

1 Potatoes are supposed to be planted in March.

2 Lettuce is supposed ....

Drill C

I suppose you'll be busy gardening in December.
  I'm hoping to find time to lift the celery.

I suppose you'll be busy gardening in ....
  I'm hoping to find time to ....

Exercise C

1 I'm hoping to find time to lift the celery in December.

2 I'm hoping to find time to ....

Drill D

I'm thinking of planting some cabbages.
  You'd better plant them in June.

I'm thinking of ....
  You'd better .... it/them in ....

Exercise D

1 If you are thinking of planting cabbages, you had better plant them in June.

2 If you are thinking of sowing beans ....

	Favourite Activities	Greatest Dislikes	Spare time Hobbies	Ambitions
Jerry Jive	spending money	working hard	playing football	to be rich
Terry Twist	driving cars	being alone	making furniture	to write songs
Ruth Rock	having parties	getting up	going fishing	to direct a film
Sue Shake	buying clothes	doing housework	painting pictures	to write a book
Roger Roll	watching films	going to bed	collecting coins	to act in films
Penny Pop	having fun	writing letters	riding horses	to stop working

Drill A

What does Jerry Jive like doing?
He loves spending money.

What does .... like doing?
He/She likes/loves/enjoys ....

Exercise A

1 Jerry Jive loves spending money.
2 Terry Twist enjoys ....

Drill B

What does Ruth Rock hate doing?
She can't stand getting up.

What does .... hate doing?
He/She hates/can't stand/can't bear to ....

Exercise B

1 Ruth Rock can't stand getting up.
2 Sue Shake can't bear ....

Drill C

What does Roger Roll do in his spare time?
He's keen on collecting coins.

What does .... do in his/her spare time?
He's/She's keen on/fond of ....

Exercise C

1 Roger Roll is keen on collecting old coins.
2 Penny Pop is fond of ....

Drill D

What does Terry Twist want to do?
He'd like to write songs.

What does .... want to do?
He/She'd like to/love to ....

Exercise D

1 Terry Twist would like to write songs.
2 Sue Shake would love to ....

1st may

WAYSIDE GARAGE LTD

Repair tyre	1	75
Clean starter motor	1	25
Check brakes	0	50
Change oil	1	50
Replace plugs	1	25
Repair horn	0	75
Check steering	0	50
Change air filter	0	50
Replace bulb	0	25
£	8	25

Drill A

Is your air filter all right now?
  Yes, I've just had it changed.

Is/Are your .... all right now?
  Yes, I've just had it/them ....

Exercise A

1 I've just had my air filter changed.

2 I've just had my tyre ....

Drill B

Did you get your brakes done?
  Yes, I had them checked yesterday.

Did you get your .... done?
  Yes, I had it/them .... yesterday.

Exercise B

1 I had my brakes checked yesterday.

2 I got my horn ....

Drill C

I'll have to get my oil changed.
  Well, it cost me one pound fifty to have mine changed.

I'll have to get my ....
  Well, it cost me .... to have mine ....

Exercise C

1 It cost me £1.50 to have my oil changed.

2 It cost me £1.25 to get ....

Shopping list

1 loaf bread
1 pkt. biscuits
2 lbs. beef
1 lb butter
2 pts milk
1 doz eggs
2 large bars chocolate
½ lb tea
1 tin soup
5 lbs potatoes
2 lbs apples
½ lb cheese

Drill A

Do we need much bread?
　One loaf will be enough.

Do we need much/many ....?
　............ will be enough.

Exercise A

1 We don't need much bread. One loaf will be enough.

2 We don't need many ....

Drill B

We need some bread, don't we?
　There's a little in the cupboard but we'd better get some more.

We need some ...., don't we?
　There is/are a little/few in the cupboard/fridge but we'd better get some more.

Exercise B

1 There is a little bread in the cupboard but we'd better get some more.

2 There are a few ....

Drill C

Are you getting any biscuits?
　We haven't got many left, so I'd better get some.

Are you getting any ....?
　We haven't got much/many left, so I'd better get some.

Exercise C

1 We haven't got many biscuits left, so I've gone out to get some.

2 We haven't got much ....

The Swan Restaurant

3 tomato soups	24
1 chicken soup	9
2 sausages	50
1 roast beef	40
1 omelette	80
4 chips	40
2 fruit salads	24
1 ice cream	9
1 apple pie	13
1 tea	5
3 coffees	21
	£2·65

Drill A

How much does a portion of chips cost?
   Ten p.

How much does an omelette cost?
   Thirty p.

How much does a/a portion/helping/plate/cup of .... cost?
   ....

Exercise A

1 A portion of chips costs 10p.

2 An omelette ....

Drill B

How many cups of tea did they have?
   One.

How many .... did they have?
   ....

Exercise B

1 They had 1 cup of tea.

2 They had ....

Drill C

What did you have to eat?
   I had tomato soup, roast beef and chips, fruit salad and coffee.
Was it good?
   Yes, it was. I liked the roast beef.

What did you have to eat?
   I had .... and ....
Was it good?
   Yes, it was/No, it wasn't. I liked/didn't like the ....

Exercise C

1 The meal was good. I had tomato soup, roast beef and chips, fruit salad and coffee. I liked the roast beef.

2 The meal wasn't very good. I had ....

Imports for 1975

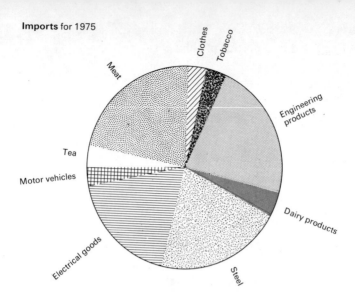

Exports for 1975

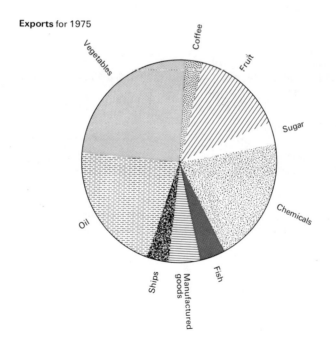

86 Section 8

Drill A

Do they import many motor vehicles?
   No, not many.

Do they import much steel?
   Yes, a lot.

Do they import much/many ....?
   Yes, a lot/No, not much/many.

Exercise A

1 They don't import many motor vehicles.

2 They import a lot of steel.

3 They ....

Drill B

Your country produces fruit, doesn't it?
   Yes, and a lot of it's exported.

Your country produces ships, doesn't it?
   Yes, but not many of them are exported.

Your country produces ...., doesn't it?
   Yes, and ..../but .... exported.

Exercise B

1 A lot of the fruit we produce is exported.

2 Not many/much ....

Drill C

We imported a lot of meat in nineteen seventy-five.
   Yes, we did. But we didn't import much tobacco.

We imported/exported a lot of .... in nineteen seventy-five.
   Yes, we did. But we didn't import/export much/many ....

Exercise C

1 In 1975 we imported a lot of meat but we didn't import much tobacco.

2 In 1975 we ....

Tomorrow's Weather

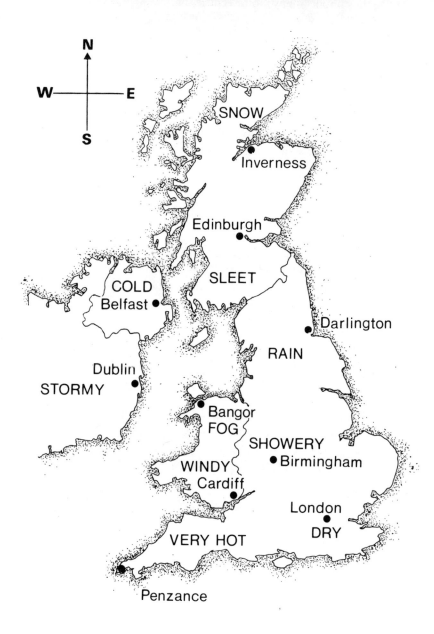

Drill A

What'll the weather be like in South Wales tomorrow?
It'll be windy.

What'll the weather be like in the north of Scotland?
There'll be snow.

What'll the weather be like in .... tomorrow?
It/There'll be ....

Exercise A

1 It will be windy in South Wales tomorrow.
2 There will be snow ....

Drill B

I'm going to Penzance tomorrow.
It said on the radio it's going to be very hot there.

I'm going to .... tomorrow.
It said on the radio it's/there's going to be .... there.

Exercise B

1 It said on the radio it's going to be very hot in the south-west of England tomorrow.
2 It said on the radio there's going to be snow ....

Drill C

Is it going to be stormy tomorrow?
Only in Southern Ireland.

Is it/there going to be .... tomorrow?
Only in ....

A Publisher's Catalogue

The Teach Yourself Series

Teach Yourself Carpentry
Teach Yourself Dressmaking
Teach Yourself Chinese Cookery
Teach Yourself Photography
Teach Yourself Russian
Teach Yourself Bridge
Teach Yourself Typing
Teach Yourself French Cookery
Teach Yourself Chess
Teach Yourself Hebrew

Drill A

I'd like to make a table.
   Why don't you teach yourself carpentry with one of these books?
   That's a good idea. I'll buy myself a copy tomorrow.
I'd like to be able to cook Chinese dishes.
   Why don't you teach yourself Chinese cookery with one of these books?
   That's a good idea. I'll buy myself a copy tomorrow.
I'd like to be able to ....
   Why don't you teach yourself .... with one of these books?
   That's a good idea. I'll buy myself a copy tomorrow.

Exercise A

1 You can teach yourself to make a table with one of these books.
2 You can teach yourself ....

Drill B

We're thinking of teaching ourselves dressmaking. Are those books any good?
   Well, Joan taught herself dressmaking in four months with one of those books.
We're thinking of teaching ourselves photography. Are those books any good?
   Well, Bill taught himself photography in two weeks with one of those books.
We're thinking of teaching ourselves .... Are those books any good?
   Well, ... taught himself/herself .... in .... with one of those books.

Exercise B

1 Joan taught herself dressmaking in 4 months with one of those books.
2 Bill taught himself ....

Drill C

I wonder if we could teach ourselves bridge?
   I'm sure we could. John and Ann taught themselves how to play bridge.
I wonder if we could teach ourselves ....?
   I'm sure we could. .... and .... taught themselves how to ....

Exercise C

1 John and Ann taught themselves how to play bridge.
2 Mary and Sue ....

APPOINTMENTS
DR BROOM

Date __12/5/76__

Morning surgery

- 9.00 Mrs Naylor
- 9.15
- 9.30 Mr Collins
- 9.45
- 10.00 Mr Grant
- 10.15
- 10.30 Mrs Fairley
- 10.45 Mr Briggs

Evening surgery

- 6.00 Mr Watson
- 6.15 Miss Banks
- 6.30 Mr Easide
- 6.45
- 7.00 Miss Temple
- 7.15 Mrs Terence
- 7.30
- 7.45 Mr Drysdale

Drill A

Is anybody coming at nine?
Yes, Mrs Naylor.

Is anybody coming at nine fifteen?
No, nobody.

Is anybody coming at ....?
Yes, .../No, nobody.

Exercise A

1 Somebody has an appointment for 9 a.m.

2 Nobody ....

Drill B

Can I see Doctor Broom at nine o'clock?
No, I'm afraid you can't; he's seeing someone else then.

Can I see Doctor Broom at quarter past nine?
Yes, you can; he isn't seeing anyone else then.

Can I see Doctor Broom at ....?
....

Exercise B

1 You can't come at 9 a.m. because Dr Broom is seeing someone else then.

2 You can ....

A Sociogram
(showing who likes who)

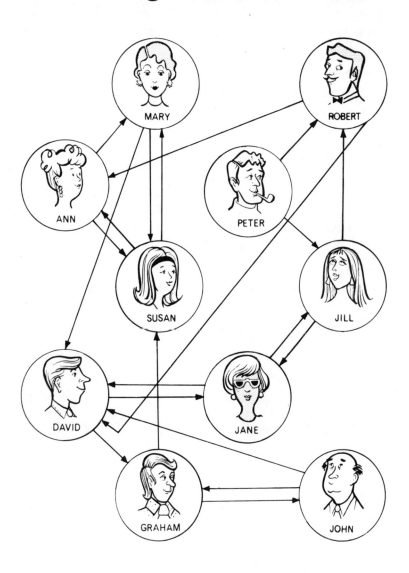

Drill A

Who does Mary like?
   David and Susan.
Who does .... like?
   ....

Exercise A

1 Mary likes David and Susan.

2 Robert ....

Drill B

Who likes Jill?
   Peter and Jane do.
Who likes ....?
   .... does/do.

Exercise B

1 Peter and Jane like Jill.

2 David and John ....

Drill C

Do John and Jane like each other?
   No, they don't.

Do Graham and Susan like each other?
   Graham likes Susan, but Susan doesn't like Graham.

Do .... and .... like each other?
   ....

Exercise C

1 John and Jane don't like each other.

2 Graham likes Susan ....

Drill D

Are Ann and Jane friends?
   No, they never talk to one another.

Are .... and .... friends?
   No, they never talk to/visit one another.

Exercise D

1 Ann and Jane never talk to one another.

2 Peter and Graham never visit ....

Section 9 95

NEWTOWN TENNIS CLUB

COURT BOOKINGS

Name	May 7	14	21	28	June 4	11	18	25	July 1	8	15	22	29	August 5	12	19	26
Mr Allison	4.00		7.00	3.00		8.00		7.00	2.00	3.00		7.00		7.00	8.00	6.00	8.00
Miss Church																	
Mr Davis			8.00	4.00				7.00						2.00			
Mr Evans	2.00	3.00	6.00	5.00	2.00	3.00	3.00	3.00	3.00	4.00	2.00	3.00	3.00	6.00	7.00	3.00	4.00
Mrs Evans		4.00	5.00	6.00	3.00		4.00	4.00		3.00	3.00	4.00		5.00	6.00	5.00	3.00
Mr George																	
Miss Johnson			8.00				5.00							2.00			
Miss Lyons	5.00	7.00	4.00	7.00	5.00	2.00	5.00	5.00	5.00	5.00	4.00	5.00	5.00	4.00	5.00	6.00	5.00
Mr Rice			3.00				8.00					3.00					2.00
Mrs Stiles																	
Mr Wales	6.00	5.00	2.00	2.00	6.00	4.00	2.00	2.00	4.00	2.00	6.00	2.00	2.00	2.00	3.00	4.00	6.00
Miss Wilson	3.00	6.00			4.00	5.00	6.00	6.00	6.00	6.00		6.00	6.00	3.00	4.00	7.00	7.00

Drill A

Is Mrs Evans a member of the tennis club?
  Yes, I often see her there.

Is Mr George a member of the tennis club?
  Yes, but I never see him there.

Is .... a member of the tennis club?
  Yes, I often/always/Yes, but I never/don't often see him/her there.

Exercise A

1 I often see Mrs Evans at the tennis club.

2 I never see Mr George ....

Drill B

Miss Lyons sometimes plays tennis, doesn't she?
  Yes, she always plays at the club.

Mr Davis sometimes plays tennis, doesn't he?
  Yes, but he doesn't often play at the club.

Exercise B

1 Miss Lyons always plays tennis at the club.

2 Mr Davis ....

Drill C

How often does Mr Rice play tennis?
  Well, he's seldom been at the club this year.

How often does .... play tennis?
  Well, he's/she's always/often/seldom/never been at the club this year.

Exercise C

1 Mr Rice has seldom been at the club this year.

2 Miss Wilson ....

SCHOOL REPORT

NAME: Linda Jackson
CLASS: 3B

MATHS	Quick to learn
ENGLISH	Intelligent work
FRENCH	Bad
SCIENCE	Careless work
HISTORY	Good work
GEOGRAPHY	Slow learner
MUSIC	Hard worker.
ART	Careful Worker
RELIGION	Satisfactory
SPORT	Enthusiastic player

Drill A

How did Linda do in French?
She did badly.

How did she do in Geography?
She learned slowly.

How did she do in ....?
She ....

Exercise A

1 Linda did badly in French.

2 She learned slowly ....

Drill B

What must Linda try to do in Science?
She must try to work more carefully.

What must Linda try to do in History?
She must try to go on working well.

What must Linda try to do in ....?
She must try to ....

Exercise B

1 In Science Linda must try to work more carefully.

2 In History she must try to ....

Electricity Consumption

	Watts
Oven	3000
Grill	2500
Fridge	100
Freezer	300
Kettle	2500
Washing machine	2500
Iron	1250
Water heater	3000
Radiator	1000
Wall fire	750
Electric blanket	80
Television	100
Vacuum cleaner	500

Drill A

How much does it cost to have a television on?
   It's not very expensive.

How much does it cost to have an iron on?
   It's fairly expensive.

How much does it cost to have .... on?
   It's very/fairly/not very expensive.

Exercise A

1 It is not very expensive to have a television on.

2 It is fairly expensive ....

Drill B

How much electricity does an oven use?
   A lot.

How much electricity does a radiator use?
   Quite a lot.

How much electricity does .... use?
   Not very much/Quite a lot/A lot.

Exercise B

1 An oven uses a lot of electricity.

2 A radiator ....

Drill C

Which uses more electricity, an oven or a grill?
   An oven uses rather more.

Which uses more electricity, a water heater or a radiator?
   A water heater uses a lot more.

Which uses more electricity, ... or ....?
   .... uses a bit more/rather more/a lot more.

Exercise C

1 An oven uses rather more electricity than a grill.

2 A water heater ....

Yesterday's Temperatures

Algiers	26	London	15
Amsterdam	14	Luxembourg	12
Athens	23	Madrid	20
Barbados	30	Malta	24
Barcelona	20	Milan	16
Belfast	13	Montreal	21
Belgrade	12	Moscow	4
Beirut	27	Munich	10
Bermuda	26	Naples	19
Berlin	11	New York	25
Brussels	13	Nicosia	29
Budapest	13	Oslo	13
Cardiff	13	Paris	14
Casablanca	20	Prague	9
Chicago	22	Rome	18
Cologne	13	Stockholm	11
Copenhagen	11	Tangier	23
Dublin	11	Tel Aviv	27
Edinburgh	11	Toronto	23
Florence	21	Tunis	28
Frankfurt	10	Venice	18
Geneva	15	Vienna	12
Gibraltar	21	Warsaw	10
Glasgow	11	Zurich	12
Helsinki	13		
Istanbul	23		

Drill A

Which was hotter yesterday, Prague or Warsaw?
Warsaw was one degree hotter than Prague.
Which was hotter/colder yesterday, ... or ....?
.... was .... hotter/colder than ....

Exercise A

1 Warsaw was 1 degree hotter than Prague yesterday.
2 Cologne ....

Drill B

Tom's in Prague.
I'm glad I'm not. It's a lot cooler than it is here.
Peter's in Gibraltar.
I wish I was. It's a bit warmer than it is here.
............'s in ....
I'm glad I'm not/I wish I was. It's a lot/a bit colder/cooler/warmer/sunnier/nicer than it is here.

Exercise B

1 It's a lot cooler in Prague than it is here.
2 It's a bit warmer ....

Drill C

Where would you like to be—Florence, Glasgow or Moscow?
I'd like to be in Florence. It's the sunniest of the three.
Where would you like to be—............, ... or ....?
I'd like/I wouldn't like to be in .... It's the warmest/hottest/sunniest/coldest/coolest of the three.

The Swan Restaurant

MENU

Tomato soup	8p
Chicken soup	9p
Roast beef	40p
Chicken	35p
Sausages	25p
Omelette	30p
Peas	9p
Beans	8p
Boiled potatoes	8p
Chips	10p
Apple pie	13p
Ice-cream	9p
Fruit Salad	12p
Tea	5p
Coffee	7p

Drill A

Would you like peas or beans?
I think peas are nicer.

Would you like .... or ....?
I think .... is/are nicer/more tasty.

Exercise A

1 I think peas are nicer than beans.
2 I think ....

Drill B

Which is cheaper, apple pie or ice-cream?
Ice-cream's cheaper.

Which is/are cheaper/more expensive, ... or ....?
............'s/are cheaper/more expensive.

Exercise B

1 Ice-cream is cheaper than apple pie.
2 Chips are ....

Drill C

Which is the cheapest drink you can buy here?
Tea's the cheapest.

Which is the most expensive/cheapest soup/main course/vegetable/pudding/drink you can buy here?
............'s/are the most expensive/cheapest.

Exercise C

1 Tea is the cheapest drink you can buy here.
2 Roast beef ....

EXAMINATION RESULTS OUT OF 100

Name	English	French	Latin	Maths	Science	History	Geog.
PETER BOLLINS	75	80	78	33	51	94	66
MARY DAVIS	79	63	65	68	62	58	67
JILL HUNTER	52	25	53	91	73	67	59
MATTHEW JAMESON	61	42	20	64	70	15	67
OLIVER KENT	83	67	76	81	92	68	61
PATRICK O'LEARY	55	58	91	43	48	78	23
DOROTHY PARTRIDGE	64	72	69	75	66	47	94
MICHAEL RAINE	58	60	55	74	68	61	53
JEAN RAMSEY	69	92	84	56	22	65	62
ELSIE SMITH	90	73	70	66	59	67	71
DAVID TRENCHARD	54	63	65	17	62	54	57
KENNETH WILSON	25	48	43	51	54	57	55

Drill A

How did Peter and Mary get on in the English exam?
Mary did better than Peter.

How did .... and .... get on in the .... exam?
.... did better/worse than ....

Exercise A

1 Mary did better than Peter in the English exam.

2 Patrick did worse than Michael ....

Drill B

Peter and David aren't very good at Maths, are they?
No, but David's worse than Peter.

.... and .... are/aren't very good at ...., aren't/are they?
Yes, and/No, but ....'s better/worse than ....

Exercise B

1 David is worse than Peter at Maths.

2 Patrick is better than Jean ....

Drill C

Who is the best in the class at English?
Elsie. She got the most marks.

Who is the best/worst in the class at ....?
.... He/She got the most/least marks.

Exercise C

1 Elsie is the best in the class at English.

2 Jill is the worst ....

Drill D

Matthew likes Maths.
Yes, but he got more marks in Science.

.... likes/hates ....
Yes, but he/she got more/less marks in ....

Exercise D

1 Matthew got more marks in Science than in Maths.

2 Kenneth got less marks in English ....

A DINNER TABLE

Mr Lansbury

Mrs Roberts   Mrs McLaren

Mr Jarvis   Mr Walker

Mrs Walker   Miss Stacey

Mr Ratcliffe   Mr Roberts

Mrs Jarvis   Miss Oliver

Mr McLaren

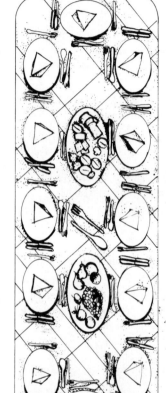

Drill A

Where's Miss Stacey sitting?
   She's between Mr Walker and Mr Roberts.

Where's Mrs McLaren sitting?
   She's next to Mr Walker.

Where's Mr Lansbury sitting?
   He's opposite Mr McLaren.

Where's .... sitting?
   He's/She's ....

Exercise A

1 Miss Stacey is sitting between Mr Walker and Mr Roberts.

2 Mrs McLaren ....

Drill B

Who's on Miss Oliver's right?
   Mr Roberts is.

Who's on ....'s right/left?
   ....is.

Exercise B

1 Mr Roberts is on Miss Oliver's right.

2 Mr Ratcliffe ....

Drill C

Who is Mr Ratcliffe sitting next to?
   Mrs Walker and Mrs Jarvis.

Who is Miss Stacey sitting opposite?
   Mrs Walker.

Who is .... sitting next to/opposite?
   ....

A Street Plan

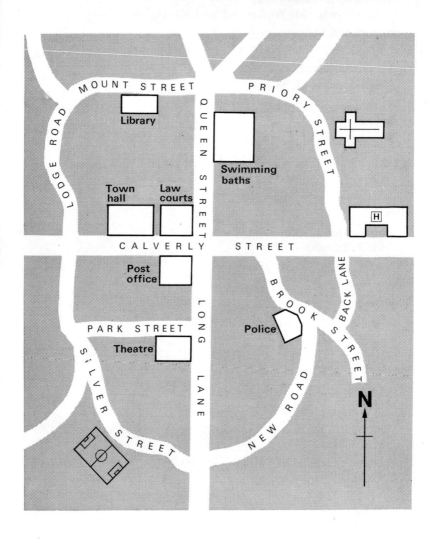

Drill A

Where's the church?
It's in Priory Street.

Where's the theatre?
It's at the corner of Long Lane and Park Street.

Where's the ....?
It's ....

Exercise A

1 The church is in Priory St.

2 The theatre ....

Drill B

How do I get from the football ground to the library?
You go north along Silver Street, straight ahead into Lodge Road, and it's on your right.

How do I get from the town hall to the police station?
You go east along Calverly Street, take the second turning on the right into Brook Street and it's on your right.

How do I get from .... to ....?
You go ...., ..., and it's on your ....

Exercise B

1 To get from the football ground to the library you go north along Silver St, straight ahead into Lodge Rd, and the library is on your right.

2 To get from ....

The Brighton Affair
by William Straiton

Lady Charlotte Banks	Sally Fraser
Sir Jasper Banks	Graham Todd
Betty (the maid)	Isobel Irvine
Charles Marsden	Reginald Davies
Paula Marsden	Barbara Willis
Daniel Marsden (their son)	Gerald Lord
Julia Brooks	Lena Anderson
Doctor Oswald	Roy Thomas
Inspector Craig	Brian Taylor
P.C. Maxwell	George Osgood

Act One   Scene 1   The Banks' summer house
                                Early evening, Tuesday
               Scene 2   The beach
                                Midnight
               Scene 3   The street outside the Marsdens'
                                Following day

Act Two   Scene 1   The doctor's
                                Wednesday afternoon
               Scene 2   The living-room of the Marsdens' house
                                Teatime
               Scene 3   The bus stop
                                Middle of the night

Act Three   Scene 1   A 27 bus
                                6 am.
                 Scene 2   The Banks' ball room
                                Afternoon

Drill A

Enjoying the play?
　Very much. Isn't Sally Fraser good as Lady Charlotte?
Yes, she is. You need a good actress in a part like that.

Enjoying the play?
　Very much. Isn't .... good as ....?
Yes, he/she is. You need a good actor/actress in a part like that.

Exercise A

1 Sally Fraser was good as Lady Charlotte.

2 Graham Todd was good ....

Drill B

Where does the first scene of Act One take place?
　In the Banks' summer house.

Where does the .... scene of Act .... take place?
　...............

Exercise B

1 The first scene of Act One takes place in the Banks' summer house.

2 The first scene of Act Two ....

Drill C

When does the first scene of Act One take place?
　In the early evening on Tuesday.

When does the .... scene of Act .... take place?
　...............

Exercise C

1 The first scene of Act One takes place in the early evening on Tuesday.

2 The third scene of Act Two ....

BIRTHDAYS

January
4th Janette (10)
22nd Kenneth (19)

February

March
15th Martin (14)

April
2nd George (5)
30th Aunt Mabel (51)

May
11th Grandma
14th Doreen (17)

June
6th Mrs Thompson
17th Frank (12)
21st Father (46)

July

August
9th Great Aunt Kate (102)
22nd Vivian (7)

September
18th Christopher (15)
19th Uncle Peter (34)
22nd Mother (39)

October
31st Aunt Jenny (47)

November
16th Mr Lewis (28)
17th Grace (3)

December
12th Oliver (9)

Drill A

Whose birthday is on the second of April?
  George's. It's his fifth birthday.

Whose birthday is on the .... of ....?
  ....'s. (It's his/her .... birthday.)

Exercise A

1 It's George's birthday on 2nd April.
2 It's Grandma's birthday ....

Drill B

Aunt Jenny's birthday and yours are in the same month, aren't they?
  No, hers is in October, but mine's in ....

............'s birthday and yours are in the same month, aren't they?
  No, his/hers is in ...., but mine's in ....

Exercise B

1 Aunt Jenny's birthday is in October, but mine is in ....
2 Doreen's birthday ....

Chicken Curry (for two people)

2 onions
½ lb apples
1 oz fat
3 tomatoes
1 spoonful curry powder
1 oz flour
1 cupful water
4 pieces chicken
¼ lb rice
1 banana

Peel and slice onions and apples. Fry for 5 mins. Add tomatoes. Fry for 5 mins. Turn heat down. Add curry powder. Stir mixture well. Fry for 5 mins. Add flour, water and chicken. Cook mixture gently for 1 hour. Boil rice for 12 mins. Serve curry with rice and banana slices.

Drill A

What do you do after peeling and slicing the onions and apples?
  You fry them for five minutes.

What do you do before/after ....?
  You ....

Exercise A

1 After peeling and slicing the onions and apples, you fry them for five minutes.
2 Before serving the curry ....

Drill B

When shall I add the tomatoes?
  When you've fried the onions and apples for five minutes.

When shall I ....?
  When/After you've ....

Exercise B

1 When you've fried the onions and apples for five minutes, you add the tomatoes.
2 After you have added the curry powder ....

A List of Cars

	Cylinders	Gears	Brakes Front / Rear		Maximum Speed	Price
Fiat 128	4	man.	disc	drum	87 m.p.h.	£972
Renault 12 Estate	4	man.	disc	drum	87 m.p.h.	£1171
Morris Marina	4	man.	drum	drum	85 m.p.h.	£941
Jaguar V 12	12	man.	disc	disc	146 m.p.h.	£3458
Ford Granada	6	aut.	disc	drum	108 m.p.h.	£2091
Volkswagen 120	4	man.	drum	drum	70 m.p.h.	£791
Mini 850	4	man.	drum	drum	72 m.p.h.	£695
MGB	4	man.	disc	drum	106 m.p.h.	£1390
DAF 33 Van	2	aut.	drum	drum	64 m.p.h.	£725
Opel Ascona	4	man.	disc	drum	93 m.p.h.	£1364
Vauxhall Ventora	6	man.	disc	drum	101 m.p.h.	£1584

Drill A

Has the Vauxhall Ventora got front disc brakes?
Yes, and it's got a six cylinder engine, too.

Has the Mini eight-fifty got automatic gears?
No, and it hasn't got disc brakes either.

Has the .... got ....?
Yes/No, and it's/it hasn't got .... too/either.

Exercise A

1 The Vauxhall Ventora has got a 6 cylinder engine and front disc brakes.

2 The Mini 850 hasn't got automatic gears or ....

Drill B

Which cars cost less than eight hundred pounds?
Three of them do; the Volkswagen, the Mini and the Daf.

Which cars have got rear disc brakes?
One of them has; the Jaguar.

Which cars............?
....

Exercise B

1 Three of the cars, the Volkswagen, the Mini and the Daf, cost less than £800.

2 One of the cars, the Jaguar ....

Drill C

I want a car that's got a six cylinder engine and costs about fifteen hundred pounds. Which do you recommend?
Well, I know somebody who bought a Vauxhall Ventora and they seem to like it.

I want a car that .... and .... Which do you recommend?
Well, I know somebody who bought a .... and they seem to like it.

Exercise C

1 If you want a car that's got a 6 cylinder engine and costs about £1500 I've got a friend who owns a Vauxhall Ventora and likes it.

2 If you want a car that can go at about 70 m.p.h. and ....

Famous People

	16th Century	17th Century	18th Century	19th Century	20th Century
ITALY	Michelangelo	Galileo		Verdi	
FRANCE		Molière Descartes	Rousseau	Pasteur Renoir	Rodin
GERMANY	Dürer		Kant Bach	Brahms Bismarck	Einstein
RUSSIA				Tolstoy Tchaikovsky	Stravinsky
ENGLAND	Shakespeare	Newton Milton		Dickens Darwin	Churchill
AMERICA			Washington	Twain	
SPAIN		Cervantes	Goya		Picasso

Drill A

Have you ever heard of Michelangelo?
 Of course I have. He was a famous sixteenth century Italian artist.

Have you ever heard of Rodin?
 Of course I have. He was a famous twentieth century French sculptor.

Have you ever heard of ....?
 Of course I have. He was a famous ....

Exercise A

1 Michelangelo was a famous 16th century Italian artist.
2 Rodin ....

Drill B

Newton was a scientist, wasn't he?
 Yes, but don't ask me what he did. I don't know anything about science.

Molière was a playwright, wasn't he?
 Yes, but don't ask me what he wrote. I don't know anything about plays.

.... was a ...., wasn't he?
 Yes, but don't ask me what he .... I don't know anything about ....

Exercise B

1 I know that Newton was a scientist, but I don't know much else about science.
2 I know that Molière ....

BBC 2

9.35 - 1.00 Open University
9.35 Political cultures; 10.05 Glasgow; 11.35 Transportation; 12.05 Quantum Theory; 12.35 Games Theory

1.50 - 6.30 Cricket; Gloucester v. Warwick

7.00 News Review for the deaf

7.25 The Sound of Dolphins with Jacques Cousteau

8.10 Scott on Food; Terry Scott and his favourite food

8.55 Music on 2; André Watts plays Bernstein, Schubert and Liszt

9.50 The Roads to Freedom, 7; dramatization of trilogy by Jean-Paul Sartre

10.35 For the Nation; Clandon Park

10.50 World Chess Championship

11.15 News Summary and weather

11.25 One Man's Week; Alan Bennett

BBC 1

6.05 News and weather

6.15 All in a day's work; a doctor's life

6.50 Sunday Service

7.25 Jack Jones in concert

8.00 Film: The Executioner; spy thriller

10.25 News and weather

10.35 Omnibus at the Proms; Brahms Piano Concerto No. 1 in D minor

11.25 International Golf; Gene Littler and Gary Player

ITV

6.05 News and weather

6.15 Young people talking; Scottish 6th-formers discuss Christianity

7.00 Songs of Praise

7.25 Doctor in Charge; medical comedy

7.55 Film: Rebel without a Cause; James Dean oldie

9.30 Who do you do?; impersonations

10.00 News and weather

10.15 A Bit of Vision; play by Charles Wood about an unhappy marriage

11.20 Eleven Plus; Russell Harty talks to Margaret Thatcher

12.05 The Bishops; Eric Wild, Bishop of Reading

Drill A

What time does *Doctor in Charge* start?
  Twenty-five past seven.

What time does .... start?
  ....

Exercise A

1 *Doctor in Charge* starts at 7.25 p.m.

2 *International Golf* ....

Drill B

Can we watch *Jack Jones* and *Scott on Food*?
  Yes, *Jack Jones* finishes at eight o'clock and *Scott on Food* doesn't start until ten past eight.

Can we watch *The Roads to Freedom* and *A Bit of Vision*?
  No, *A Bit of Vision* starts at quarter past ten and *The Roads to Freedom* doesn't finish until twenty-five to eleven.

Can we watch .... and ....?
  Yes/No, ... finishes/starts at .... and .... doesn't start/finish until ....

Exercise B

1 We can watch *Jack Jones* and *Scott on Food* because *Jack Jones* finishes at 8.00 p.m. and *Scott on Food* doesn't start until 8.10 p.m.

2 We can't watch *The Roads to Freedom* and ....

A Telephone Directory

Abbot D. 36, Brook St	Clacton	92184
Abbs E.M. 3, High St	Braintree	1482
Abercrombie G. Hill Farm	Nayland	827
Able G.K. 2, Park Lane	Ipswich	73882
Abraham Mrs E. 238, Meadow Way	Colchester	90012
Ackerley I.R. 44, Fifth Avenue	Ipswich	41723
Ackroyd Mrs M.E. 11, Highfield Rd	Sudbury	3662
Acton R. 37, St Edmunds Rd	Clacton	98036
Adams T. 181, Sidegate Lane	Colchester	44311
Adamson Miss K.L. Rose Cottage	Great Bentley	423
Adcock J.A. 263, Spring Lane	Colchester	63892
Addington L.A. 42, High St	Manningtree	3031
Addison A.E. 27, Fitzwalter Rd	Stowmarket	5255
Adkins Mrs A.O. 17, Clive Ave	Colchester	38918
Agnew B.M. Manor Hall	Tiptree	6318
Aikman Miss H.M. 4, Benton St	Ipswich	63285
Ainsley S. 13, Mayfield Gardens	Frinton	8829
Airey Mrs A. Oak Tree Cottage	Woodbridge	3631
Aitken G. 21, The Avenue	Clacton	86142
Albin G.S. 34a North St	Colchester	43844

Drill A

Mr Able lives in Ipswich, doesn't he?
  Yes, at two, Park Lane.

.... lives in ...., doesn't he/she?
  Yes, at ....

Exercise A

1 Mr Able lives at 2, Park Lane, Ipswich.

2 Mrs Ackroyd ....

Drill B

Shall I give Mr Albin a ring?
  Yes. His number is Colchester four three eight double four.

Shall I give .... a ring?
  Yes. His/Her number is ....

Exercise B

1 Mr Albin's telephone number is Colchester 43844.

2 Miss Aikman's ....

Drill C

Do you know Mr Adcock?
  Isn't he the man who lives in Spring Lane?

Do you know Mrs Airey?
  Isn't she the woman who lives at Oak Tree Cottage?

Do you know ....?
  Isn't he/she the man/woman who lives in/at ....?

Exercise C

1 Mr Adcock is the man who lives in Spring Lane.

2 Mrs Airey ....

INDEX

(Numbers refer to page numbers; letters refer to drills or exercises)

adjectives: (comparative of) 103ab, 105ab, 107bd; (possessive) 115a; (order of) 121a; (superlative of) 103c, 105c, 107c
adverbs: (comparative of) 107a; (of degree) 101; (of frequency) 97; (of manner) 99
after 117
ago 27d
ahead of v. *behind* 17c
allowed to 51c, 57b
a lot of v. *much/many* 87
anybody 93a
anyone 93b
apposition 19d
as v. *like* 113a

be (present perfect) 35c; (simple past) 21d, 23b; (simple present) 9a; (simple present v. simple past) 9b, 23a, 49a
been to 25ab, 27ac
before 117a
behind v. *ahead of* 17c
be not to 57c

can 51b, 54ab
comparative of adjectives 103ab, 105ab, 107bd
comparative of adverbs 107a
conditional I 67a, 69ab
conditional II 55c, 67b, 69c
conditional III 67c, 69d
conjunctions: *after, before, when* 117; *in case* 55b; *unless* 55d
could 53c, 61b

dates 115
derived nouns 121b

each other 95c
either v. *too* 119a
else 93b

few v. *little* 83b
fewest v. *most* 33a
for (length of time) 35b
future continuous 37c, 41b, 47b
future passive 65c
future perfect 47c, 69a
future sense of present continuous 37b, 39ac, 41a, 89b

future tenses 37-41
future with *going to* 37ad, 39c, 89bc
future with *will* 37cd, 41c, 47c, 89a

gerunds 77acd, 79 abc, 117a
going to 37ad, 39c, 89bc

had better 59b, 77d
have/have got (present tense) 11, 13c; (past tense) 21c
have as full verb: (v. *have got*) 13c; (present perfect) 25c; (simple present) 13a; (simple present v. simple past) 13b
have something done 81
have to 51, 55d
how many 85b
how much 85a

if: see 'conditional'
in case 55b
indefinite pronouns 93
indirect speech 71, 73
infinitive 75c, 77c, 79bd; (passive) 77b
interrogative *who* 95ab
irregular comparison 107
it v. *there* 89

least v. *most* 107c
less v. *more* 107d
like v. *as* 113a
little v. *few* 83b

many v. *much* 83ac
many/much v. *a lot of* 87
mass and unit 83-87
may 55a
might 55c
modals: *be not to* 57c; *can* 51b, 53ab; *could* 53c, 61b; *have to* 51, 55d; *may* 55a; *might* 55c; *must* 59a; *mustn't* 53a, 57a; *needn't* 55d; *ought to* 53b, 55b, 59bc; *shall* 61bc; *should* 55a, 59c; *will* (future) 37cd, 41c, 47c, 89a; *will* (request) 61a
more v. *less* 107d
most v. *fewest* 33a; v. *least* 107c
much v. *many* 83ac
much/many v. *a lot of* 87
must 59a
mustn't 53a, 57a

needn't 55d
nobody 93a
noun phrases 121a
numerals (cardinal) 125ab; (*once, twice*, etc) 35c; (ordinal) 115a

of (partitive) 85a, 119b
once, twice, etc. 35c
one another 95d
order of adjectives 121a
ought to 53b, 55b, 59bc

partitive *of* 85a, 119b
passive 63-65; infinitive 77b; present continuous 63c; present continuous (future sense) 39b; present perfect 63bc, 65c; simple past 63ab, 65ab; simple present 65b; *will* 65c
past continuous 29a; v. present continuous 49b; v. simple past 29bc
past perfect after *wish* 49c
past perfect v. present perfect 33b; v. simple past 31bc
past tense: see simple past, past continuous
possessive adjectives 115a
possessive pronouns 115b
prepositions: *ago* 27d; *ahead of* v. *behind* 17c; *as* v. *like* 113a; *for* (length of time) 35b; *since* 27c, 35a, 47a
prepositions of place 109, 111, 113b; of time 113c; + gerund 77ad, 79c, 117a
present continuous 17, 19c; passive 63c; v. past continuous 49b; v. simple past 23b; v. simple present 19bd
present continuous with future sense 37b, 39ac, 41a, 89b; passive 39b; v. present perfect and simple past 43a
present perfect 25, 27c, 33a, 35c; after *when, before* and *after* 37d, 117b; passive 63bc, 65c; v. past perfect 33b; v. simple past 27ad, 43b, 49c; v. simple past and present continuous with future sense 43a; v. simple past and *will* 47d; v. simple present 45bc
present perfect continuous 35ab, 47a
present tense: see simple present, present continuous

pronouns 89-95; (indefinite) 93; (possessive) 115b; (reciprocal) 95cd; (refelxive) 91; (relative) 19d, 119c, 125c

reciprocal pronouns 95cd
reflexive pronouns 91
relative pronouns 19d, 119c, 125c
reported speech 71, 73

-self/-selves (reflexive pronouns) 91
shall 61bc
should 55a, 59c
simple past 21, 27b, 31a, 85c; of *be* 21d, 23b; of *have* 21c; passive 63ab, 65ab; v. past continuous 29bc; v. past perfect 31bc; v. present continuous 23b; v. present perfect 27ad, 43b, 49c; v. present perfect and present continuous with future sense 43a; v. present perfect and *will* 47d; v. simple present 13b, 23, 49a
simple present 15, 19a; of *be* 9a; of *have* 11, 13; passive 65b; v. present continuous 19bd; v. present perfect 45bc; v. simple past 13b, 23, 49a; v. *used to* 45a
since 27c, 35a, 47a
somebody 93a
someone 93b
superlative of adjectives 103c, 105c, 107c

there v. *it* 89
time 15, 17, 123
too v. *either* 119a

unless 55d
used to v. simple present 45a

when (conjunction) 117b
who (interrogative) 95ab
will (future) 37cd, 41c, 47c, 89a; passive 65c; v. present perfect and simple past 47d
will (request) 61a
will be doing 37c, 41b, 47b
will have done 47c, 69a
wish + past perfect 49c
would like 39c, 53c, 79d